CHILTON'S GUIDE to
HOME ENERGY SAVINGS

CHILTON'S GUIDE
to
HOME ENERGY SAVINGS

LEWIS VAUGHN

Drawings by
DOROTHY BACINO
NAN EVERSON
KATHY VAUGHN

CHILTON BOOK COMPANY
Radnor, Pennsylvania

Copyright © 1982 by Lewis Vaughn
All Rights Reserved
Published in Radnor, Pennsylvania 19089, by Chilton Book Company
and simultaneously in Canada by VNR Publishers,
1410 Birchmount Road, Scarborough, Ontario M1P 2E7

Library of Congress Cataloging in Publication Data

Vaughn, Lewis.
    Chilton's guide to home energy savings.

    Bibliography: p. 213
    Includes index.
    1. Dwellings—Energy conservation—Handbooks,
manuals, etc.   I. Chilton Book Company.
II. Title.
TJ163.5.D86V38   1982   643.7   80-70335
ISBN 0-8019-7231-0   AACR2
ISBN 0-8019-7019-9 (pbk.)

Manufactured in the United States of America

        1 2 3 4 5 6 7 8 9 0   1 9 8 7 6 5 4 3 2

To KATHY *and* ERIN

Contents

Insulation: Curbing the Cash Flow   65

Acknowledgments

MANY THANKS to those special people who gave time and talent to help this book into being, who proved that good friends are better than gold: Dorothy Bacino, Robert Bingaman, Daniel Boxler, Prudence Ellis, Harold Ellis, Nan Everson, June Mento, Thomas Pitcherella, Mary Ann Pontician, Michael Shapiro, Wendy Shelton, Linda Spink, Mary Swick, Ron Swick, Frank Tucker, Darryl Waller.

Introduction

THIS is a field manual for those who have declared war on the shocking costs of home energy—those who can't take another sky-high heating bill, those whose homes leak energy dollars by the hundreds, those who are fed up with appliance operating costs that maul the family budget. For homeowners, apartment dwellers, and students of conservation, this volume is basic training in the best energy-saving techniques.

Here you'll find only the *proven* technologies you can put on-line right now, practical technologies that yield measurable energy savings. Our emphasis is on essential information: how specific conservation schemes work, how much they cost, and how much money they can save. We've stripped the text clean of technical jargon and wasted words, for the shortest distance between two minds is plain language.

Chapter 1 gives you the background you need to make your *own* weatherization decisions about your *own* situation. You learn about the crucial variables in your home's energy equation, including heat loss, heat gain, conduction, convection, radiation, infiltration, U-values, R-values, and more. Then you find out how to give your home an energy audit, a top-to-bottom inspection that reveals where and why you're wasting energy dollars.

In chapter 2 you discover how to capitalize on all that data you dig up: how to calculate your heat losses, size up your heating costs, do a benefit/cost analysis of weatherization options, and derive your own customized package of weatherization investments. The chapter is your conservation road map, helping you to stay on the path of smart weatherization tactics and steer clear of the ploys that steal your money.

Chapter 3 takes a close look at one of those fuel-saving maneuvers: installing thermal insulation. What's the stuff made of? How much does your home need? Where and how do you install it? Do you need vapor barriers? What safety precautions should you take during installation? Should you hire an insulation contractor? To insulate properly you have to ask these questions, and this chapter provides plenty of straight answers.

And because the air leaks in your abode can cost you a fortune in heating and cooling costs, chapter 4 is your guide to the best leak-stoppers available: effective weatherstripping and caulking. After reading the guide, you will be able to walk into any hardware store and confidently select the perfect stripping or caulking for your needs. Considering the scores of different materials available for plugging household air seepage, that's a handsome feat. You also get lots of tips on how to install all those sealers, everything from tubular gaskets to automatic door bottoms to long-lasting silicone caulk.

Your windows and doors squander more heat than equal areas of insulated wall. To help you slow those losses, chapter 5 tells you about the features, effectiveness, cost, and installation of the most useful window and door insulators. Storm windows, interior single-pane kits, thermal shades, pop-in shutters, foam-core doors—you learn about all these and more.

In chapter 6 you see how to slash heating and cooling costs right at the source: your heating or cooling system. You can save a lot of money by retrofitting or replacing your low-efficiency boiler or furnace, and this chapter shows you how to do it without losing your shirt. You also find out how to trim energy costs through proper heating or cooling maintenance. You may be surprised at how much cash you can bank by doing the right kind of system-tinkering at the right time. And if you're thinking about some alternatives to conventional heating or cooling plants, survey the sections on the airtight wood stove, the heat pump, and the kerosene heater. These can offer welcome relief from the bruising price increases of conventional fuels.

The last chapter demonstrates that you can whittle your electric bill down to size without sacrificing your comfort. You learn how to curb the electrical appetites of your biggest watt-users: your refrigerator, freezer, range, oven, dishwasher, washing machine, and clothes dryer. And you master the art of sensible lighting, the techniques that afford you all the home lighting you need at the lowest possible price.

CHILTON'S GUIDE to
HOME ENERGY SAVINGS

CHAPTER ONE

Home Weatherization: Getting Your Bearings

CARL SIMPSON was so angry when he walked through his front door that he didn't even stop to wipe the snow from his shoes. He had just been jolted into a rage by the evening paper and his monthly heating bill. The paper's big headline was FUEL OIL COSTS TO JUMP 8%—AGAIN! The bill said, "Pay this amount: $200."

The headline stung, but the bill stung harder because he had just installed a brand-new furnace. He paced the floor and fumed. He knew he had to weatherize, to plug up the leaks, to use fuel more efficiently. But the more he thought about it, the more confused he became. Should I insulate the attic and weatherstrip the doors? Or would it be better to install storm windows? I can't afford to do everything, so what do I do first? And how do I figure out which conservation measures will save me the most money over the long haul?

Carl Simpson's angry bewilderment illustrates the classic predicament of many modern homeowners. They're ready and willing to weatherize, but they simply don't know how to begin. They're asking the kinds of questions that Carl did, but they're not getting any answers. They're hurting enough financially to try investing in home conservation, but they don't have the kind of information that makes wise investments possible.

In short, they need to get their bearings. They need a no-nonsense seminar in the basic concepts of smart weatherization. And they need to know more about the patients they're trying to cure—their houses. They need to read this chapter. It's a guide to all those weatherization ideas that have been so much in the news lately: heat loss, R-values, conduction, convection, infiltration, and others. It also tells how to give a house an energy checkup, to see what kind of defenses it has (or doesn't have) against fuel waste.

With this background, you can analyze your energy situation in even more detail, in chapter 2. You can actually calculate the amount of energy you're losing and where. You can determine the cost-effectiveness of the most important weather-fighting projects. And you can establish weatherization priorities that will match your budget and lifestyle.

This analytic approach to weatherization is essential—without it, you're out in the cold. Unless you're willing to take a hard look at your house, your energy use, and your weatherization options, you run the risk of money-wasting investments. Unfortunately, it happens all the time. Someone adds more insulation to his attic and then discovers that most of his energy dollars were going right out the windows—and still are. Someone else hires a contractor to blow insulating cellulose into his walls and later realizes that the payback period is 30 years.

HEAT FLOW

Heat flow is the fundamental concept of home weatherization. Understand heat flow and you understand why weatherization is necessary, why conservation measures save money, and why some energy saving techniques are better than others.

Let's begin with a simple definition: Heat flow is the transfer of heat energy from one place to another. The movement of heat from a stove burner to a saucepan is one example. Heat flow from the sun to the sidewalk is another. So is the heat flow from your fireplace to the winter air. A corollary to our definition is that heat always flows from warm areas to cool ones, and its rate of travel depends in part on the temperature difference between the areas. The greater the temperature difference, the faster the flow.

In winter, heat flows from your home heating system to the cold outside air. The heat generated indoors does not fade away or self-destruct. It just leaves—through your walls, doors, ceiling, floors, and windows. In other words, you have winter fuel bills because you're heating the Great Outdoors! In the summer, of course, the transfer of heat is reversed. Warmth from outdoors seeps into the cooler interior of your house, and the job of your air conditioner is to pump the hot air back where it came from.

Obviously, the purpose of weatherization is to reduce this winter *heat loss* and summer *heat gain*. And, believe me, the rewards for cutting your house's heat flow can be enormous. Experts say that by employing simple conventional weatherization techniques, you can cut your energy consumption by 50% or more!

Figure 1-1 shows where typical heat losses occur in an average one-story uninsulated house. As you can see, most heat is lost through the ceiling or roof. Windows and doors lose about as much as walls, even though total wall area is much greater than window and door area. And a great deal of heat escapes by infiltration; that is, through cracks in the foundation, crevices around doors and windows, and openings such as the chimney.

An analogy may help put heat loss in perspective. If you pour water into a bucket with holes in it, that water may trickle out as fast as you splash it in, in which case the water level stays the same. But if you plug up some of those holes, you can reduce your pouring rate because the water won't leak out as quickly as before. Now, your house is a lot like the bucket. If your home's heat loss equals the amount of heat given off by your furnace, the indoor temperature will remain constant. So to ensure a comfortable indoor temperature, your furnace must replace every bit of heat your house

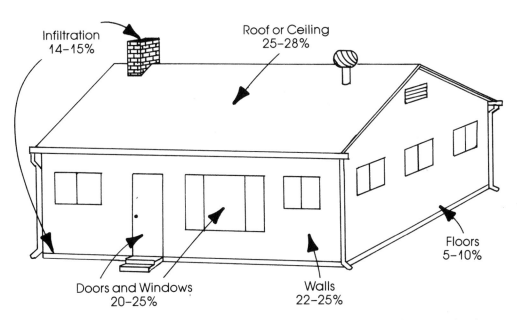

Fig. 1-1. Heat losses of an average single-story uninsulated house. In general, a two-story house loses less heat through the roof, but more through the walls, than a one-story house.

loses. If you plug up some holes (with insulation, weatherstripping, and so on), your furnace won't have to work as hard. You can keep your thermostat set where it always was, but your heating plant won't kick on nearly as often.

If you know your house's heat loss, you can calculate how much heating capacity you must have, how much weatherizing you need to do, and how much money you can save through heat-stopping tactics. I'll discuss heat loss calculations more thoroughly in chapter 2, because first we need to examine the three ways that heat flows: conduction, convection, and radiation.

Conduction

Conduction is the transfer of heat energy from molecule to adjoining molecule. When heat is conducted, it travels like an ink stain on a blotter, creeping from particle to particle. If you place one end of an iron rod in a flame, soon the heat will travel through the rod to the other end. That's conduction.

But what happens if you slip a copper rod into that flame? Heat will travel to the other end much faster. Why? Because different materials conduct heat at different rates. Or, to put it another way, some things have a higher conductivity than others. Materials with high conductivity are called *conductors*; those with low conductivity are called *insulators*.

What does all this have to do with your house and those infernal fuel bills? Plenty. Chances are, your house loses most of its heat by conduction (and, in the summer, gains a lot of heat the same way). If your home is uninsulated, as much as 75% of your heat could be flowing right through the floor, the windows, the outer doors, the walls, and the ceiling. What's more, the rate of heat flow through those surfaces depends, in part, on what they're made of. As we'll see, some materials are better heat-stoppers than others.

U-values and R-values

All of this theory about conduction can be put to work in a practical way by employing *U-values* and *R-values*. These factors help you quantify conduction heat losses and differentiate between conductors and insulators. And that kind of information allows you to make intelligent decisions about how to retard heat flow.

A U-value, or *coefficient of heat transmission*, is a measure of the rate of heat flow (conduction) through the things we build houses out of—walls, floors, shingles, plaster, glass, and so on. To be more precise, a U-value represents the amount of heat transmitted per hour through a square foot of building material(s) when there is a 1°F temperature difference between the air on each side of the material(s). If you know the U-value for one of your house's outside walls, and there is a 1°F temperature difference between indoors and outdoors, then you know precisely how much heat one square foot of that wall is gaining or losing each hour. The U-value tells the tale.

If you multiply that U-value by the number of square feet in your wall area (minus window and door areas), you'll find out how much heat is flowing hourly through the entire wall when there's 1°F temperature difference. If that difference is, say, 20°F instead of 1°F, the rate of heat conduction is proportionately greater—twenty times greater.

U-values are expressed in *British thermal units per hour (Btuh).* The Btu is a standard unit of heat measurement, defined as the amount of heat needed to raise 1 pound of water 1°F. It's about equal to the heat given off when a wooden match ignites and burns to ashes. If your walls have a U-value of 2.85, that means they're losing (or gaining) 2.85 Btuh through each square foot of wall area for every 1°F inside/outside temperature difference.

U-values measure heat conduction; R-values measure heat resistance. In other words, R-values, or *thermal resistance factors,* are yardsticks to help you assess a material's ability to resist, or retard, heat flow. Wallboard with an R-value of 2 is a better heat-stopper than plywood sheathing with an R-value of 1. And 2-inch-thick pine paneling has more than twice the insulating power of an 8-inch-thick concrete block wall, because the R-value of the pine is 2.50 and that of the concrete is 1.04.

As you might have guessed, the U-value of a material is the inverse of the R-value (U = 1/R). For example, gypsum board with an R-value of 0.45 has a U-value of 2.22 (1/0.45). The 2.22 is shorthand for 2.22 Btuh; the 0.45 is a simple ranking of resistance power, without units of measurement.

You can add insulators to insulators and add up their R-values to get a higher resistance rating. For example, you can calculate the R-value of a building section (wall, floor, etc.) by adding up the R-values of the section's components. A roof consisting of shingles (R = 0.44), $\frac{1}{2}$-inch plywood deck (R = 0.63), and 6 inches of mineral wool insulation (R = 19.00) has an R-value of 20.07 (0.44 + 0.63 + 19.00 = 20.07). The three tables at the end of this chapter show R-values for common building materials, windows, and doors.

Convection

To a homeowner, the second most important method of heat flow (after conduction) is *convection.* When you're sitting in your favorite easy chair and suddenly a cool draft raises the hair on your neck, you're experiencing the bedevilment of convection. And the cold air flowing in under the front door? Yes, that's convection at work, too. Technically, convection is the transfer of heat by the movement of heat-laden liquids or gases (including air), and this movement affects your indoor comfort in two ways.

First, there is the draft problem already mentioned—the problem of chilly convection currents. Because warm air from your heating system is less dense than cool air, it rises, wafting slowly upward, letting the cool air move in to replace it. Gradually it loses some of its heat, becomes more dense, and falls, mixing with the cooler air below. Soon this cooler air absorbs heat from your heating plant and the cycle of rising and falling is repeated. If your walls have large enough interior air cavities, convection currents will even swirl around between framing studs. On cool days convection eddies can make you shiver or send you running to turn up the thermostat.

Second, there's the bugbear of air infiltration, the leakage of air into your house through cracks in your exterior walls, crevices around windows and doors, and other openings. Air infiltration is actually a kind of convection current; indeed, infiltration eddies help feed the whirling air that's always in your house. I'm discussing infiltration separately, however, because in wintertime it can not only give you a chill, but it can also steal heat from your home. In fact, an uninsulated house can lose as much as a third of its heat through infiltration. In winter, cool air leaks in, pushes the warm air out, and forces your furnace to take up the slack. Every cubic foot of cool air that seeps in needs 0.02 Btu to raise its temperature 1°F. To put it another way, that cubic foot of cold air needs 39 Btuh to raise its temperature to 65° when it's 30° outside; that adds up to 936 Btus every day. And the harder the wind blows, the faster the winter slips in and the Btu's slip out.

All the above is, of course, a strong argument for weatherstripping and caulking. But, you may ask, isn't some infiltration necessary? Certainly. Your house must breathe to prevent structural damage caused by condensation. And for you to stay healthy, your house must undergo about one complete air change per hour. Most older homes, however, have a complete air change two to three times per hour, which means they're wasting a lot of energy. Yes, your house must breathe, but don't let that thought keep you from sealing up the leaks. You can install tight-fitting storm windows, caulk every crevice, install airlocks around the exterior doors, put building paper under the siding and still have a house that takes big healthful breaths around the clock. As long as you ensure proper attic ventilation and sufficient venting for your combustion appliances (oil furnaces, gas stoves, kerosene heaters, and so on), you can safely weatherize from roof to cellar.

Radiation

The third method of heat flow is *radiation*, the transfer of heat through open space via electromagnetic waves. When heat radiates from a source (the sun, an open flame, a light bulb), it travels like light, in straight lines, and always toward cooler areas. Radiant heat warms only the surfaces that impede its journey. You get a dramatic lesson in radiant heat every time you're in a room with a burning fireplace. Heat from the flames goes to the surfaces in the room, leaving a nip in the air, a warm glow on your face, and a chill on your back.

Your house loses heat by radiation in winter and gains heat by radiation in summer. This heat flow, however, is hard to measure, and often insignificant. But radiation does affect your indoor comfort, especially in the winter. Your body, at 98.6°F, radiates heat, and the cooler your surroundings, the more radiant heat will flow from you. So if your house walls are cold because there isn't enough insulation in them to keep out the chill, your body will radiate heat to them. They will be, in effect, sucking warmth right from your skin. The result: you'll have to crank up the thermostat to compensate for the shiver down your spine. This is another argument for a weathertight house.

Heat Loss Through Walls

So there you have it: a homeowner's course in conduction, convection, and radiation. Before we move on to other things, let's look at how the three modes of heat flow can interact in uninsulated exterior walls. As you can see from Figure 1-2, heat travels from your furnace to your sidewalls by convection and radiation. It then moves through the inside wall surfaces (usually wallboard) by conduction. If the wall cavity is uninsulated, heat continues to the outside wall coverings via all three modes: convection currents move about between the wall studs, thermal radiation speeds across the air spaces, and warmth conducts right through the framing members.

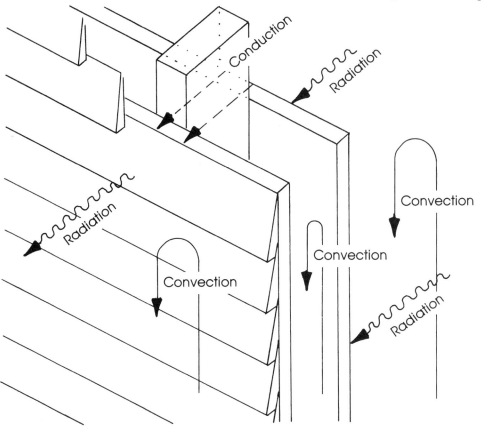

Fig. 1-2. Heat flow through an uninsulated sidewall.

The heat that penetrates the wall's outside surface exits by radiation and convection. You'll find the same kind of thermal flow in uninsulated roofs and ceilings.

HOME ENERGY INSPECTION

Before you start weatherizing your house, it's best to have a full understanding of the status quo. Your house may be more energy efficient than you think or it may be wasting more fuel than you thought possible. At any rate, you'll never know the real story until you look around.

Your investigation should include determining insulation levels, finding air leaks, checking building materials, and measuring barriers to heat flow. The payoff for all this snooping is a storehouse of data that allows you to calculate your heat losses. As every reputable insulation contractor knows, calculating heat losses is the only way to *precisely* assess your house's wintertime energy efficiency and the value of conservation measures.

Your home energy inspection will be more valuable if you organize the information you gather. The Energy Work Sheets are designed to do just that. If you fill them in as you conduct your inspection, you'll be able to analyze your data more easily. In this chapter we'll fill in the tops of the Work Sheets, the blanks that ask for area measurements and R-values. Don't worry about the bottom half of the Work Sheets for the time being. We'll work through those calculations in the next chapter.

Attic or Roof

Before you can calculate heat loss through the top of your house, and before you buy insulation to stuff up there, you have to measure the area of your overhead barrier to heat flow—the building section(s) that should separate heated air from winter chill. If you have a common flat roof, you know that your upper barrier should be the roof itself. To find its area, just measure its length and width and multiply the two numbers. (Be careful, though, to subtract the area of roof overhangs, and ignore chimneys and vents.) If you have a typical mansard roof, your topside heat barrier should be the sloping sides and horizontal deck(s) that make your mansard a mansard. Simply measure the length and width of each of those segments, compute their areas, add them up, and subtract the area of any windows.

Your roof may have structural complexities (dormers, turrets, and so on) that leave you wondering what to measure and what to ignore. So take note of the First Law of Barrier Inspection: if an architectural structure divides heated areas from unheated, it's a heat buffer and should be treated as such.

If you don't have a flat or mansard roof, chances are you have an attic. Which part of your attic should be your heat barrier? That is, what section up there should you measure? The answer depends on whether your attic is finished or unfinished. If it's finished (Figure 1-3), you probably want to keep the winter cold out of it. In that case, the heat shield should include the end walls, knee walls, roof-ceiling (attached to roof rafters and collar beams), and ceiling boards fastened to attic floor joists outside the finished area. If your attic is unfinished and floorless (Figure 1-4), your barrier should be the ceiling of the living area immediately below the attic (the ceiling boards spanning the attic floor joists). If it's unfinished and has a floor, there are two possibilities: The heat buffer can be the floor itself (which means

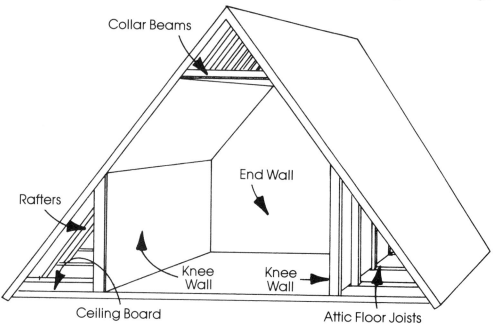

Fig. 1-3. A finished attic. "Finished" usually means gypsum board walls and a plank floor.

there should be insulation under the floor covering) or the attic "ceiling" (which means there should be insulation between the rafters).

Wherever your topside barrier is, you can find its area by using our standard formula: length × width = area. Just remember, (1) you can compute the area of nonrectangular surfaces by breaking them down into a composite of rectangles; (2) the area of flat roofs and attic floors is usually equal to the first-story floor area below them; (3) you should subtract any window area from the area of attic walls (you can ignore vents, though); and (4) Work Sheet 1 is waiting to receive all the data.

There's a good chance you're wondering how an attached garage, heated porch, or adjoining workshop figures into a roof or attic inspection. Indeed, the big question is how *any* house adjunct should be treated in a barrier inspection. The answer goes back to our First Law: any architectural structure that separates heated space from unheated is a heat buffer and should be measured, scrutinized, and weatherized. How this principle applies to inspection of house additions or extensions is best defined by example. Let's say you have an unheated two-car garage nestled on one end of your two-story house. The garage ceiling is actually the heat barrier for the living area above and should therefore be included in the floor inspection (Work Sheet 3). The wall dividing heated house and unheated garage is really an exterior wall, and should be considered part of the sidewall inspection (Work Sheet 2). The door joining garage and interior room is supposed to keep out the cold and should be listed right along with other exterior doors in Work Sheet 4. And if the garage is heated? Its only barriers should be the surfaces that stand against the cold: the outer doors and walls.

What's your topside heat barrier made of? What's the R-value of its insulation? What's the R-value and thickness of each barrier component? To conduct a thorough upper barrier inspection is to ask these questions. And, as you'll see later, getting the answers is worth the trouble.

There are two approaches to investigating the composition of your roof (or any other building section): the easy way and the hard way. The easy way means calling the contractor who put up your house and asking him what materials he used in its construction. If he gives you the information you need, and there have been no structural or composition changes since

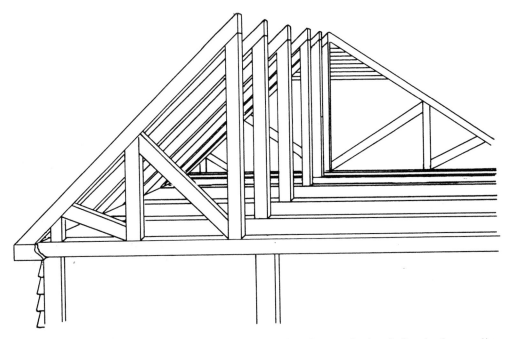

Fig. 1-4. An unfinished attic. No floor—and plenty of room for insulation between the joists.

initial building, you're set. You can complete most of Work Sheet 1 and the other Work Sheets from your easy chair. But if this approach doesn't get you all the data you need, you'll have to try the hard way: a thorough, first-hand inspection.

Inspecting the makeup of your roof can take you from five minutes to one hour, depending on how skillful you are and how accessible your roof's components are. (You'll want to note material and thickness on your Work Sheet as you go.) First, check the exterior covering. Is it a solid layer of gravel or other materials? Clay tiles? Asphalt shingles? Cedar shakes? Finding the answer to that first question will not only help you grapple with heat loss but also will tell you whether you should bother climbing up on the roof. If you discover that you have a seamless roof exterior, you may as well continue the roof inspection from the underside. To find out what's under a seamless covering, you'd have to cut it, which is a big mistake for anyone who wants a leakproof roof. If your roof is blanketed with tiles or shingles, however, you can easily loosen one up to see what's underneath. You'll probably find an underlay (roofing paper of felt), and under that some kind of sheathing or decking. (Getting at any sheathing or decking calls for slitting the underlay—easily repaired with tape or sealant.) You won't have any trouble finding out what that decking or sheathing is made of, but you may have difficulty determining its thickness. A useful energy inspection rule is, when you can't accurately measure the thickness of a heat-retarding material, guess. The information in this section should help keep your guessing informed.

Your outside inspection of rooftop layers should stop when you can't go any deeper without drilling holes; continue your examination from below, from inside your house. This exploration will mean you'll have to inspect any ceiling board or panelling attached to the rafters or decking. You may also have to remove a board or panel to get to the other roof layers. But whatever you do, be sure to check for insulation. If it's there, measure its depth. Chapter 3 will help you determine what kind it is and whether it has a vapor barrier. And don't forget to check it for water damage, which invariably reduces the R-value of any heat-stopper.

You'll want to be on the lookout for something else, too: air. Air has insulation value, especially when it's enclosed by airtight materials. If your roof (or any other barrier) has a layer of air inside between solid materials, you should measure the thickness of the gap. Be sure to record your finding on the Work Sheet, in the U- and R-value portion. You should also be aware of a barrier's insulating air films. Most barriers have two heat-retarding air films, one coating the outdoor surface, the other coating the indoor surface. These thin blankets of air are usually less than an inch thick, but that's enough to help slow the passage of heat. (A barrier surface that butts against the ground, however, doesn't have an air film.) You don't inspect these invisible air films, of course, but you should note them on the proper Work Sheet (U- and R-value section), so you can assign air film R-values when the time comes.

Assaying the composition of your attic heat barrier—whether floor, ceiling, or end wall—can be as easy or as difficult as checking a roof's makeup. The rules are the same for both kinds of inspections: (1) investigate the depth, type, and condition of any insulation you find; (2) guesstimate the thickness of buffer components when necessary; and (3) record your data. To inspect the formation of your attic floor, you'll have to pry up a few floor boards. (And remember, they're part of the barrier, too.) Uncovered attic "floors" don't have an access problem, but trying to scrutinize your finished attic barrier is another matter. To see how knee walls, ceiling, and end walls are put together, you may have to cut access holes (chapter 3 will show you how). To check out the ceiling boards outside the finished area, you'll probably need to do some crawling around.

Note that because the composition of your finished attic barrier is not uniform (for example, the components of the end walls differ from those of the outer ceiling boards), you'll have to record the materials and area for each discrete part of the buffer so that you can accurately calculate your barrier loss later on. Simply compute the heat loss for each barrier segment and add up your answers. Of course, you can use this procedure on any other nonuniform barrier you have.

I know what you're thinking: how do you ascertain the R-value for each ingredient in your heat barrier? Table 1-1 should help you there. If you need additional R-value data, try the *ASHRAE Handbook of Fundamentals* (available at your library) or your local builders' association.

Exterior Walls

Once you know how to determine the area of your attic or roof barrier, you know how to figure out the area of your other heat shields, including your exterior walls. Just keep this in mind: (1) it's usually easier to measure exterior walls outdoors than indoors, and (2) your exterior wall barrier extends from the foundation (or foundation wall) to the overhead heat

Energy Work Sheet 1: Roof and Attic

UPPER BARRIER AREA

_____ $\times$ _____ = _____ sq. ft.

_____ $\times$ _____ = _____ sq. ft.

_____ $\times$ _____ = _____ sq. ft.

_____ $\times$ _____ = _____ sq. ft.

_____ sq. ft. Total Attic or Roof Area

BARRIER U- AND R-VALUES

Material	R-Value
_____	_____ [1]
_____	_____
_____	_____
_____	_____
_____	_____
_____	_____
_____	_____
_____	_____
_____	_____
_____	_____ [2]

_____ Total R-Value

_____ Total U-Value (U = 1/R)

ANNUAL TRANSMISSION HEAT LOSS

U $\quad\times\quad$ A $\quad\times$ 24 hours $\times\quad$ D $\quad$ = Annual Transmission Heat Loss

_____ $\times$ _____ $\times$ 24 hours $\times$ _____ = _____ Btu

▪ ANNUAL BARRIER HEATING COSTS

Annual Transmission Heat Loss $\times$ Cost of Fuel Per Btu = Annual Barrier Heating Costs

_____ $\times$ \$_____ = \$_____

---

[1]If applicable, insert indoor air film R-value here.
[2]If applicable, insert outdoor air film R-value here.

buffer. Need to know the area of a triangular shape? It's one-half the base times the height. The base is any side of the triangle; the height is the perpendicular distance from the base to the opposite peak. The figures you obtain should be recorded in Work Sheet 2.

Inspecting the composition of your exterior walls is usually a half-hour job. If they have a removable outer covering (siding, shingles, shakes), you can dislodge some of it to get a look at what's underneath. You may find some rigid insulation or a special backing for the outer covering. One thing you're almost sure to run into is some sort of sheathing "blanket" over building board. It usually isn't necessary to slit the blanket to check the board, for you can easily inspect the board from inside the house.

The best place to begin an in-house inspection of those sidewalls is at a switch cover, light fixture, or electrical outlet. But before you even think of tinkering with those gadgets, turn off the power to your house at the main fusebox or circuit breaker panel. Then, and only then, remove one of the cover plates or fixtures. That should allow you to peer into the wall cavity. To get a clear view you may have to use a flashlight. If insulation is in there, try to measure its thickness with a ruler, and try to determine its type (Figure 1-5). You'll also want to check for a vapor barrier, that nonporous sheeting (usually polyethylene or foil) that prevents moisture buildup in

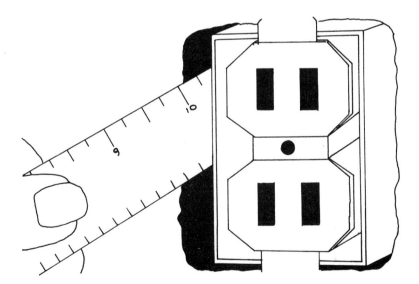

Fig. 1-5. After you take off the cover plate, you should be able to see into the wall cavity. If you need more room to see, you can cut away some of the wallboard around the outlet, as long as the cover plate will later conceal your handiwork.

the cavity and cuts infiltration to zero. Look for such sheeting between the stud area and wallboard, that is, on the indoor side of insulation. Also scrutinize the building board, any air gap, and the wallboard. Pay particular attention to any plaster because it's a big infiltration-stopper.

Heating or cooling registers in your sidewalls, special vents, or built-in fans are all potential access holes for insulation inspection, but they're last-resort possibilities. The ground rules for tinkering with them are (1) don't tear up anything that can't be easily replaced, (2) don't remove anything you can't put back, and (3) don't hesitate to consult the nearest building professional.

When you complete Work Sheet 2 and do the calculations, you'll have a darn good idea how many Btu's seep through your exterior walls each heating season. That data will help you determine, among other things, whether those walls need more heat-impeding capability. There is, however, another way to find that out, a ball-park estimate method that tells you nothing more than whether you should add insulation. Not how much, just whether. On a cool day, when the outdoor temperature is at least 20°F less than the indoor temperature, attach a room thermometer to one of your interior partition walls. Wait awhile, then check the reading. Next, transfer the thermometer across the room to an exterior wall. Attach it; wait; take a reading. If the difference between the two readings is more than 1.5°F per each 10°F of indoor/outdoor temperature difference, the exterior wall needs insulation. For example, let's say the outdoor temperature is 40°F and your partition wall is 68°F. That means the indoor/outdoor temperature difference is 28°F. If the reading on your exterior wall (in the same room as the partition wall) is 62°F, the difference between the two indoor readings is 6°F, which is more than 4.2° ($1.5° \times 2.8 = 4.2°$). So that outside wall needs insulation.

This thermometer trick does not relieve you of making a thorough wall inspection. Even if you know your sidewalls are insulated to their maximum capacity, you will still benefit by examining their size and composition. Without a good wall inspection, you can't compute your total annual or total hourly heat loss, and those facts can help you make a host of important home energy decisions. Those decisions include what your heating system capacity should be, what percentage of your annual heat loss each weatherization strategy should save, whether your present energy saving schemes will be adequate when fuel prices jump again, and whether your house is as energy efficient as one that meets FHA minimum standards.

Infiltration can be a major source of heat loss through exterior walls. (On the other hand, air leaks through roofs, ceilings, and floors are less significant and much harder to quantify. Plug the holes, but forget about computing their losses.) If you doubt the importance of sidewall air seepage, you may become a believer when you calculate your own walls' infiltration losses (Work Sheet 2). At any rate, while you're snooping, it would pay you to check for cracks, even if your sidewalls have a vapor barrier. Where there's a chink, there's the possibility of moisture damage, if not heat loss. Where are you most likely to find those holes in your house's armor? Around exterior wall vents and fans; in siding, bricks, and stucco; where the sidewalls and roof meet; around water faucets and electrical apparatus; between the sidewalls and foundation or crawl space perimeter walls; around sidewall-mounted air conditioners; and where dissimilar sidewall coverings meet or overlap. Obviously, to check out most of these spots you'll have to do an appreciable amount of outdoor inspecting, but you'll need to do a little indoor investigating, too. From inside your house you can look for daylight around sidewall air conditioners, fans, and vents, or between sidewalls and the foundation. For the moment, you can ignore those cracks around your doors and windows; tend to those when you do a separate door-and-window inspection (Work Sheet 4).

The Floor and Below

Before beginning your floor inspection, decide what your lower heat barrier is. Is it your crawl space? Your floor? Your basement? It depends, of course, on where you want to draw the line between heated areas and unheated areas. If you have neither a crawl space nor a basement nor any other below-grade structure, your floor is your barrier, and it should be insulated. But if you have an open area below your floors, you have more than one place where a heat shield could be. Here's what I mean. If you have a basement or similar "underbuilding," you can either heat it or leave it to the cold. If you heat it, its walls and floor should be your barrier, bolstered as necessary to keep the warmth in. If you don't heat it, the floor above it will be your barrier. (In especially cold climates, that floor buffer usually needs insulation to keep the chill down below where it belongs; elsewhere, insulation is optional because heat loss to the basement is minimal.) If you have a crawl space, choose your heat shield: either the crawl space perimeter or the floor above it. In mild-winter areas, a closed-off crawl space is enough to keep heat loss to a trickle and the crawl space perimeter is barrier enough.

Energy Work Sheet 2: Exterior Walls

EXTERIOR WALL AREA

_____ × _____ = _____ sq. ft.

_____ × _____ = _____ sq. ft.

_____ × _____ = _____ sq. ft.

_____ × _____ = _____ sq. ft.

_____ sq. ft. Total Exterior Wall Area

WALL U- AND R-VALUES

Material	R-Value
_____	_____ [1]
_____	_____
_____	_____
_____	_____
_____	_____
_____	_____
_____	_____ [2]

_____ Total R-Value

_____ Total U-Value (U = 1/R)

ANNUAL TRANSMISSION HEAT LOSS

U   ×   A   × 24 hours ×   D   = Annual Transmission Heat Loss

_____ × _____ × 24 hours × _____ = _____ Btu

ANNUAL INFILTRATION HEAT LOSS

C   ×   S   ×   Q   × 24 hours ×   D   = Annual Infiltration Heat Loss

0.018 × _____ × _____ × 24 hours × _____ = _____ Btu

ANNUAL BARRIER HEAT LOSS

Annual Transmission Heat Loss + Annual Infiltration Heat Loss = Annual Barrier Heat Loss

_____ + _____ = _____ Btu

▪ ANNUAL BARRIER HEATING COSTS

Annual Barrier Heat Loss × Cost of Fuel Per Btu = Annual Barrier Heating Costs

_____ × $_____ = $_____

---

[1] If applicable, insert indoor air film R-value here.
[2] If applicable, insert outdoor air film R-value here.

But in cold regions—and places where you need lots of outdoor air in your crawl space to control moisture—your lower barrier should be your floor. At any rate, before you make a final decision about where your lower barrier is and isn't, you should read the section in chapter 3 on "Insulating Crawl Space Walls."

Inspecting the top and sides of your house is one thing; probing the bottom is another. A lower barrier inspection has to take into account factors that do not apply to other kinds of snooping. When you inspect your other barriers, you invariably measure area, examine construction materials, and check for air gaps because you need to know all that to compute heat loss. But when you scout out your lower buffer, the kind of inspection you do depends on what you inspect.

If your barrier is a floor above a crawl space, you should gauge the floor's area and composition *and* check its exposure to winter. This is because its heat loss depends on how well it's protected from cold as well as how big it is and what it's made of. Surveying exposure means determining the tightness of the crawl space perimeter. Energy Work Sheet 3 will translate the degree of tightness into a numerical value. You can use the value to fine-tune your heat loss calculations (see the Work Sheet instructions) and to give you a good idea of how weatherproof your perimeter is. You'll find that an unshielded crawl space doesn't do a thing for energy conservation (exposure factor of 1.0). A crawl space with some protection against wind reduces heat loss through the floor to 80% of what it would be without shielding (exposure factor of 0.8); a crawl space with a tight skirt or foundation wall and less than 2 feet of perimeter exposed above ground reduces heat loss to 50% (exposure factor of 0.5); and a crawl space with a windtight foundation wall reinforced with insulation ($R = 4.0$) cuts heat loss to 30% (exposure factor of 0.3).

As you check the perimeter, you might note any infiltration seepage it has—in case you want to do some leak-plugging later on. Such note-taking, of course, would be a good idea in just about any kind of lower barrier inspection.

Inspecting a crawl space perimeter barrier is mostly a matter of measuring its area and determining its makeup. But you must be careful to subtract the area of vents and access holes from the total buffer area. You have to understand the influence of the crawl space "floor," too. That ground below does steal a small amount of heat from the floor above. But the loss is difficult to ascertain because there's so little available data on ground temperatures and U-values. So stick to inspecting the perimeter only, calculating your heat loss from the information you get, and remembering that your loss figures will be a little short—but accurate enough to be useful.

If your lower barrier is a slab floor, you can skip area measurements, composition checks, and most of Work Sheet 3. A quick investigation to see if your floor has perimeter insulation is all that's necessary. (Perimeter insulation is usually rigid and goes around the foundation wall, or from the slab edge to underneath the slab a few feet.) You see, slab floors are a special case. Knowing their area and composition won't tell you much because you can't accurately compute their heat loss using that data alone. Figuring their losses involves a special equation (which is a needless complication here) and comprehensive slab heat loss data (which is scarce). A slab floor usually loses only about 10% of a house's heat, and perimeter insulation can cut slab loss by 33% or more. As rough as they are, those numbers can help you do a fair job of guesstimating slab losses and potential insulation savings. Guesstimates of heat loss and heating costs are always useful, and always worth recording on your Work Sheets.

The inspection method for a basement-wall-and-floor barrier depends on whether the basement is above ground or below. If it's more or less above, you inspect much as you would for a crawl space perimeter barrier. That is, you measure the wall area (subtracting the area of windows and vents), determine the wall composition, and ignore the floor (for the same reason you disregard a crawl space "floor"). If the basement is below ground, you determine the placement and R-value of any perimeter insulation, and that's as far as you go. A scarcity of data on ground temperatures and other factors makes our heat loss calculations impossible, and therefore a full inspection is unnecessary. But if you at least know how much insulation the basement barrier has, you can determine if heat-blocking reinforcements are called for. And if you understand that such barriers can lose about 15% of your house's heat, you can rough out a heat loss figure.

Windows and Doors

Your windows and doors take up so little space that their effect on your household energy equation is insignificant. Right? Don't you believe it! Chances are, your windows and doors take up as much as 40% of your house's perimeter wall area and lose more heat per square foot of surface than any other barrier you have. Even weatherstripped windows with extra glazing can lose five to ten times as much heat as an uninsulated wall of equal area. And the figures for doors aren't much better.

Energy Work Sheet 3: The Floor and Below

LOWER BARRIER AREA

_____ × _____ = _____ sq. ft.

_____ × _____ = _____ sq. ft.

_____ × _____ = _____ sq. ft.

_____ × _____ = _____ sq. ft.

BARRIER U- AND R-VALUES

Material	R-Value
_____	_____ [1]
_____	_____
_____	_____
_____	_____
_____	_____
_____	_____
_____	_____ [2]

_____ Total R-Value

_____ Total U-Value (U = 1/R)

ANNUAL TRANSMISSION HEAT LOSS

U × A × 24 hours × D = Annual Transmission Heat Loss

_____ × _____ × 24 hours × _____ = _____ Btu

If your barrier is a floor above a crawl space, multiply the above loss figure by the value that most closely reflects your floor exposure:

House on posts or pillars with no perimeter protection   1.0

House on posts or rocks with some protection against wind   0.8

Tight skirt or foundation wall around perimeter and less than 2 feet of wall or skirt exposed above grade   0.5

Tight foundation wall with insulation (R = 4.0) on inside or outside of wall   0.3

▪ ANNUAL BARRIER HEATING COSTS

Annual Transmission Heat Loss	× Cost of Fuel Per Btu =	Annual Barrier Heating Costs
_____	× $_____ =	$_____

---

[1] If applicable, insert indoor air film R-value here.

[2] If applicable, insert outdoor air film R-value here.

Obviously, your windows and doors deserve close scrutiny. Because they're your biggest heat wasters, measuring and examining them should be a top priority. Such an inspection can tell you more about their physics and economics than some insulation contractors can.

Does the window portion of Work Sheet 4 look formidable? Don't worry; it seems more complicated than it is. Actually, completing this portion of the Work Sheet will probably take you less than 20 minutes. The biggest part of your window inspection is determining the size and R-value of your glazing, and the Work Sheet is organized to help you do just that. To calculate window transmission heat loss, you have to know the total area of all the glazing of a given R-value, so the Work Sheet helps you group glazing accordingly.

If you take a look at Table 1-2, you'll see why there are blanks for air space data in Work Sheet 4. The air space between fixed sheets of glazing makes a big difference in R-value, in heat-retarding power. You already know that confined ("dead") air makes a good insulator. Well, that air space between window glazing can be a more potent heat-stopper than the glazing itself. So be sure to measure that dead air. If Table 1-2 doesn't list the R-value you need, you can figure out a rough estimate from the values given.

Even in window inspection you have to observe our First Law: check out every piece of glazing that separates heated areas from unheated. Cellar windows, skylights, glazing in exterior doors, attic windows, garage windows—they're all candidates for close examination. You should add the R-values of any interor insulating devices (thermal shades, insulating shutters) to glazing R-values, but ignore window sashes, meeting rails, or mullions (pane dividers) when figuring window area or R-value.

Measuring your outer (barrier) doors takes only a few minutes, and deciding what they're made of should take even less. If you really can't determine their composition, check with your local building supply store. Table 1-3 lists R-values for common doors, and Table 1-1, the R-values for building materials, will help you concoct R-values for uncommon ones, such as those with insulating panels, garage versions, and special designs.

After you gauge the size and R-values of your doors and windows, you'll want to give them an infiltration inspection. To compute their infiltration heat loss, you need to know their crack lengths and their general physical condition. For calculation purposes, "crack length" is narrowly defined. For a double-hung window, it's the inside perimeter of the frame plus the length of the meeting rail; for a window with pivoted sashes, it's the total perimeter of the movable sections; for a door, it's simply the edge perimeter. Record the crack length of each of your doors and windows in Work Sheet 4. As far as that Work Sheet infiltration formula is concerned, assessing the "general physical condition" of your windows and doors involves nothing more than checking for weatherstripping and noting type of construction and frame-to-sash(-door) fit. In the section on calculations you'll see just how well these bits of information can aid your weatherization efforts. You may even discover that some of the crevices around your doors and windows are losing more Btu's than the doors and windows themselves!

Obviously, gathering facts for computing window and door infiltration doesn't require an extensive inspection. But you should look a little further if you're thinking about doing a caulking job later on. That means hunting for air-seeping cracks where window casings adjoin walls, where window glass connects with sashes, between door frames and house walls, and around door jambs. If you're not sure whether a crevice leaks air, you can hold a candle flame near it. If the flame flutters, there's air seepage.

A Postscript

Your local utility company may provide a low-cost energy inspection service. For $15 or $20, a trained professional will go through your house, top to bottom, and ask you about your day-to-day use of rooms, entrance doors, and major appliances, and your room heating requirements. All this information is fed on the spot into a computer. The output is recommendations about where to insulate and what to do to cut your fuel bills. The remainder is up to you. And that remainder is in chapters 3–7 of this book.

One advantage of the service is that you get recommendations on energy-saving measures tailored to your house with no effort on your part. The disadvantage is that the inspector gets to know your house inside and out, but you don't. Doing your own inspection and analysis lets *you* decide on the most effective energy-saving measures you can afford.

Energy Work Sheet 4: Windows and Doors

WINDOWS

Single Glass (R-value = _____; U-value = _____)

_____ × _____ = _____ sq. ft.   crack length _____ ft.
_____ × _____ = _____ sq. ft.   crack length _____ ft.
_____ × _____ = _____ sq. ft.   crack length _____ ft.
_____ × _____ = _____ sq. ft.   crack length _____ ft.
_____ × _____ = _____ sq. ft.   crack length _____ ft.
_____ sq.ft. Total Area

Double Glass

			Air Space	R-value	U-value	Crack Length
_____ × _____ =	_____ sq.ft.		_____ in.	_____	_____	_____ ft.
_____ × _____ =	_____ sq.ft.		_____ in.	_____	_____	_____ ft.
_____ × _____ =	_____ sq.ft.		_____ in.	_____	_____	_____ ft.
_____ × _____ =	_____ sq. ft.		_____ in.	_____	_____	_____ ft.
_____ × _____ =	_____ sq.ft.		_____ in.	_____	_____	_____ ft.

Single Glass with Storm (R-value = _____; U-value = _____)

_____ × _____ = _____ sq.ft.   crack length _____ ft.
_____ × _____ = _____ sq.ft.   crack length _____ ft.
_____ × _____ = _____ sq.ft.   crack length _____ ft.
_____ × _____ = _____ sq.ft.   crack length _____ ft.
_____ × _____ = _____ sq.ft.   crack length _____ ft.
_____ sq.ft. Total Area

Triple Glass

			Air Spaces	R-value	U-value	Crack Length
_____ × _____ =	_____ sq.ft.		_____ in.	_____	_____	_____ ft.
_____ × _____ =	_____ sq.ft.		_____ in.	_____	_____	_____ ft.
_____ × _____ =	_____ sq.ft.		_____ in.	_____	_____	_____ ft.
_____ × _____ =	_____ sq.ft.		_____ in.	_____	_____	_____ ft.
_____ × _____ =	_____ sq.ft.		_____ in.	_____	_____	_____ ft.

(Continued on next page)

ANNUAL WINDOW TRANSMISSION HEAT LOSS

U × A × 24 hours × D = Annual Window
                                Transmission Heat Loss

_____ × _____ × 24 hours × _____ = _____ Btu

_____ × _____ × 24 hours × _____ = _____ Btu

_____ × _____ × 24 hours × _____ = _____ Btu

_____ × _____ × 24 hours × _____ = _____ Btu

_____ × _____ × 24 hours × _____ = _____ Btu

_____ Btu Total Annual
        Window Transmission
        Heat Loss

ANNUAL WINDOW INFILTRATION HEAT LOSS

C × L × Q × 24 hours × D = Annual Window
                                    Infiltration Heat Loss

0.018 × _____ × _____ × 24 hours × _____ = _____ Btu

0.018 × _____ × _____ × 24 hours × _____ = _____ Btu

0.018 × _____ × _____ × 24 hours × _____ = _____ Btu

0.018 × _____ × _____ × 24 hours × _____ = _____ Btu

0.018 × _____ × _____ × 24 hours × _____ = _____ Btu

_____ Btu Total
        Annual Window
        Infiltration
        Heat Loss

TOTAL ANNUAL WINDOW HEAT LOSS

Total Annual Window   Total Annual Window   Total Annual Window
Transmission Heat Loss + Infiltration Heat Loss =   Heat Loss

_____ + _____ = _____ Btu

DOORS

			R-value	U-value	Crack Length
_____ × _____ = _____ sq.ft.			_____	_____	_____ ft.
_____ × _____ = _____ sq.ft.			_____	_____	_____ ft.
_____ × _____ = _____ sq.ft.			_____	_____	_____ ft.
_____ × _____ = _____ sq.ft.			_____	_____	_____ ft.

(Continued on next page)

ANNUAL DOOR TRANSMISSION HEAT LOSS

U   X   A   X 24 hours X   D   =   Annual Door Transmission Heat Loss

_____ X _____ X 24 hours X _____ = _____ Btu

_____ X _____ X 24 hours X _____ = _____ Btu

_____ X _____ X 24 hours X _____ = _____ Btu

_____ X _____ X 24 hours X _____ = _____ Btu

_____ Btu Total Annual Door Transmission Heat Loss

ANNUAL DOOR INFILTRATION HEAT LOSS

C   X   L   X   Q   X 24 hours X   D   =   Annual Door Infiltration Heat Loss

0.018 X _____ X _____ X 24 hours X _____ = _____ Btu

0.018 X _____ X _____ X 24 hours X _____ = _____ Btu

0.018 X _____ X _____ X 24 hours X _____ = _____ Btu

0.018 X _____ X _____ X 24 hours X _____ = _____ Btu

_____ Btu Total Annual Door Infiltration Heat Loss

TOTAL ANNUAL DOOR HEAT LOSS

Total Annual Door Transmission Heat Loss   +   Total Annual Door Infiltration Heat Loss   =   Total Annual Door Heat Loss

_____ + _____ = _____ Btu

TOTAL DOOR-WINDOW HEAT LOSS

Total Annual Window Heat Loss   +   Total Annual Door Heat Loss   =   Total Door-Window Heat Loss

_____ + _____ = _____ Btu

▪ ANNUAL WINDOW HEATING COSTS

Total Annual Window Heat Loss   X Cost of Fuel Per Btu =   Annual Window Heating Costs

_____ X $_____ = $_____

(Continued on next page)

■ ANNUAL DOOR HEATING COSTS

Total Annual Door Heat Loss × Cost of Fuel Per Btu = Annual Door Heating Costs

_____ × \$_____ = \$_____

■ ANNUAL DOOR·WINDOW HEATING COSTS

Total Door-Window Heat Loss × Cost of Fuel Per Btu = Annual Door-Window Heating Costs

_____ × \$_____ = \$_____

Table 1-1
R·Values for Common Building Materials

Material	R-Value
BUILDING BOARD	
Gypsum or plaster board, $\frac{1}{2}$ inch	0.45
Plywood, $\frac{1}{2}$ inch	0.63
Plywood, $\frac{3}{4}$ inch	0.94
Sheathing, regular density, $\frac{1}{2}$ inch	1.32
Wood fiberboard	1.82 per inch
BUILDING PAPER	
Vapor, permeable felt	0.06
Vapor barrier, 2 layers of mopped felt	0.12
Vapor barrier, plastic film	0.00
FLOORING	
Carpet and fibrous pad	2.08
Carpet and rubber pad	1.23
Wood subfloor, $\frac{25}{32}$ inch	0.98
Cork tile, $\frac{1}{8}$ inch	0.28
Terrazzo, 1 inch	0.08
Tile (asphalt, linoleum, vinyl, rubber)	0.05
INSULATING MATERIALS	
Mineral wool, blanket or batt	3.12 per inch
Fiberglass board	4.35 per inch
Corkboard	3.75 per inch
Wood fiber, blanket or batt	4.00 per inch
Expanded polyurethane, board or slab	6.25 per inch
Expanded polystyrene, board or slab	4.05 per inch
Acoustical tile, $\frac{1}{2}$ inch	1.19
Mineral wool (loose fill)	3.80 per inch
Perlite (expanded loose fill)	2.85 per inch
Sawdust or shavings	2.22 per inch
Vermiculite (expanded)	2.20 per inch
Cellulose fiber (loose fill)	4.05 per inch

Table 1-1
R·Values for Common Building Materials (*Continued*)

Material	R-Value
Roof insulation, preformed for use above deck, $\frac{1}{2}$ inch	1.39
1 inch 1 inch	2.78
2 inches 2 inches	5.26

MASONRY

Material	R-Value
Cement mortar	0.20 per inch
Concrete or stone	0.08 per inch
Brick, common	0.20 per inch
Concrete block (solid, oven dried)	0.11 per inch
8 inches thick, 2 cores	1.04
8 inches thick, filled cores	1.93

PLASTER

Material	R-Value
Cement plaster (sand aggregate)	0.20 per inch
Gypsum plaster (lightweight aggregate), $\frac{1}{2}$ inch thick	0.32

ROOFING

Material	R-Value
Asbestos-cement shingles	0.21
Asphalt roll roofing	0.15
Asphalt shingles	0.44
Builtup roofing, $\frac{3}{8}$ inch	0.33
Wood shingles	0.94

SIDING

Material	R-Value
Wood shingles, 16 inches, $7\frac{1}{2}$-inch exposure	0.87
Wood shingles with insulating backer board, $\frac{5}{16}$ inch	1.40
Asphalt roll siding	0.15
Asphalt insulating siding, $\frac{1}{2}$-inch board	1.46
Wood drop siding, 1 by 8 inches	0.79
Wood bevel siding, lapped, $\frac{1}{2}$ by 8 inches	0.81

WOOD

Material	R-Value
Maple, oak, and similar hardwoods	0.91 per inch
Fir, pine, and similar softwoods	1.25 per inch

AIR FILMS AND SPACES

Material	R-Value
Outdoor air film	0.17
Indoor air film, ceiling or roof nonreflective	0.61
reflective	1.32
Indoor air film, vertical barrier, nonreflective	0.68
reflective	1.70
Indoor air film, floor, nonreflective	0.92
reflective	4.55
Air space, roof or ceiling, $\frac{3}{4}$ inch	
nonreflective surfaces	0.87
one surface reflective	2.23
Air space, vertical barrier, $\frac{3}{4}$ inch	
nonreflective surfaces	1.01
one surface reflective	3.48
Air space, floor, $\frac{3}{4}$ inch	
nonreflective surfaces	1.02
one surface reflective	3.55

Table 1-2
R-Values for Windows

Glazing	R-Value
Single glass	0.88
Double glass, $\frac{3}{16}$-inch air space	1.45
$\frac{1}{4}$-inch air space	1.54
$\frac{1}{2}$-inch air space	1.72
Single glass with storm window, 1- to 4-inch air space	1.79
Triple glass, $\frac{1}{4}$-inch air spaces	2.13
$\frac{1}{2}$-inch air spaces	2.78
Single plastic sheet	0.92
Plastic bubble skylight, single walled	0.87
double walled	1.43

Table 1-3
R-Values for Common Doors

Door	R-Value
Solid wood 1 inch	1.56
$1\frac{1}{4}$ inches	1.82
$1\frac{1}{2}$ inches	2.04
2 inches	2.33
1 inch with wood storm	3.33
$1\frac{1}{4}$ inches with wood storm	3.57
$1\frac{1}{2}$ inches with wood storm	3.70
2 inches with wood storm	4.17
1 inch with metal storm	2.56
$1\frac{1}{4}$ inches with metal storm	2.94
$1\frac{1}{2}$ inches with metal storm	3.03
2 inches with metal storm	3.45
Steel with urethane core	2.50
Steel with styrene core	2.13

CHAPTER TWO

Home Energy Calculations: Zeroing in on Savings

AFTER you measure and examine your heat barriers, and after you fill up the Work Sheets with hard facts, you're ready to put all those figures to work. You're ready to look at your house from a different perspective—the mathematical perspective. Numbers can talk, and what they have to say about your house might surprise you. They might even save you some money.

FIGURING YOUR ENERGY LOSSES

This section will help you compute your transmission heat losses, your infiltration heat losses, your total annual heat loss, your annual heating costs, and your design heat load. It's the job of the next section to show you how to use those figures to make energy-wise decisions and avoid dead-end weatherization options.

Most homeowners have nothing but cooperative heat barriers—barriers that are accessible, barriers whose heat loss can be readily computed. So it is to those people I've addressed the next few pages. As for those of you who have inscrutable heat shields (like slab floors or below-grade basements), a guesstimate of heat loss is better than nothing. And those percentages of typical barrier losses given on page 20 are the key to usable ballpark figures.

Transmission Heat Loss

Calculating the transmission heat loss of your barriers is a simple matter because the heat loss formula on the Work Sheets makes it simple. And you already know more about that formula than you think. Here it is in its leanest form:

(Equation 1)
$$H_{tr} = U \times A \times (T_i - T_0)$$

where H_{tr} = heat transmitted per hour (Btuh)

U = U-value of building section (Btuh)

A = area of building section (square feet)

$(T_i - T_0)$ = temperature difference between indoor and outdoor air (°F)

U is the backbone of the formula. You'll recall that the U-value tells you how much heat is transmitted hourly through a square foot of a building section when there is a 1°F temperature difference between the air on each side of the section. That means if you want to compute the heat that passes hourly through a section larger than 1 square foot and with a temperature difference greater than 1°F, you simply multiply the U-value times the larger area and temperature difference. For example, let's say one of your exterior walls has a U-value of 0.20, an area of 200 square feet, and an indoor/outdoor temperature difference of 30°F. All you have to do to figure out your wall's hourly heat loss is make one quick calculation: $0.20 \times 200 \times 30 = 1200$ Btuh. And, of course, this is precisely the multiplication you do when you use Equation 1.

So if you're curious about how many Btu's you're losing each hour through one of your barriers, let Equation 1 tell you. It's easy enough to determine indoor/outdoor temperature differences. And if you've completed the top half of the Work Sheets, you already know your barriers' area and U-values. (Remember, the U-value is the inverse of the R-value. So to find out the U-value of a barrier, add up the R-values of its components and divide the sum into 1.00.)*

But what about your *annual* heat loss through a barrier? Equation 1 can't tell you that, but the expanded version of Equation 1 can:

(Equation 2)
$$H_{tr} = U \times A \times 24 \text{ hours} \times D$$

---

*If you use Equation 1 to compute the hourly heat loss through a floor over an unheated basement or a ceiling below an unheated attic, keep in mind that the "outdoor" temperature is really just the temperature of the unheated space. And that unheated space may be considerably warmer in winter than the outdoors. If you think that's true of your cold basement or attic, reduce the T_0 value. Often the average of the true outdoor temperature and T_i is a reasonable T_0.

where H_{tr} = heat transmitted annually (Btu) and D = annual degree days. U and A are the same as before. Notice that $(T_i - T_0)$ of Equation 1 is replaced by 24 hours × D. You see, when you multiply U × A × 24 hours, you get the amount of heat transmitted through a section in one day when there is an indoor/outdoor temperature difference of 1°F. And when you multiply all that by D (annual degree days), you factor in all the average temperature differences for all the days of the year. Result: heat transmitted annually.*

The degree day is one of the most useful concepts the fuel industry ever came across. A degree day represents a situation in which outdoor temperatures average 1°F below indoor temperature for 24 hours. So if the outdoor temperatures average 5°F below your indoor temperature for a full day, 5 degree days accumulate. Your total annual degree days is a measure of all your average indoor/outdoor temperature differences throughout the year. Finding that bit of data for your own climate is as easy as reading Table 2-1. Yes, energy people have amassed degree day figures for every part of the country, and they've standardized them by always assuming an indoor temperature of 65°F, a minimum comfort level.

Incidentally, knowing your degree days helps you do more than just squeeze Equation 2 for heat loss figures. Because your heating system must make up the difference between your indoor and outdoor temperatures, your degree day numbers accurately reflect your average fuel consumption. That means you can use degree day data to make reliable comparisons concerning your heating fuel needs. For example, if Table 2-1 tells you you'll have 100 degree days in October and 1000 in February, you know that you'll probably burn ten times more Btu's in February than in October. Or if you live in an area with 1000 annual degree days and you're going to move someplace ranking in the 5000 range, you can expect to use five times more heating energy in your new home. And to spend five times the fuel dollars.

So now that you know the story about degree days, you can compute the annual transmission losses for your barriers. (See the sample calculation in Figure 2-1.) And after that, you can figure your house's total annual transmission loss by simply adding up all those barrier losses. Your answer will loom in the millions of Btu's.

---

*To use Equation 2 to calculate the annual heat loss through a floor over an unheated basement or a ceiling below an unheated attic, you may have to shave D to compensate for warmer "outdoor" temperatures in the unheated space in winter. If your unheated basement or attic is generally a lot warmer in winter than the outdoors, consider reducing D by 25% or more.

Table 2-1
Average Degree Days (Base 65°)

State and Station	July	Aug.	Sep.	Oct.	Nov.	Dec.	Jan.	Feb.	Mar.	Apr.	May	June	Annual
ALABAMA													
Birmingham	0	0	6	93	363	555	592	462	363	108	9	0	2551
Huntsville	0	0	12	127	426	663	694	557	434	138	19	0	3070
Mobile	0	0	0	22	213	357	415	300	211	42	0	0	1560
Montgomery	0	0	0	68	330	527	543	417	316	90	0	0	2291
ALASKA													
Anchorage	245	291	516	930	1284	1572	1631	1316	1293	879	592	315	10864
Annette	242	208	327	567	738	899	949	837	843	648	490	321	7069
Barrow	803	840	1035	1500	1971	2362	2517	2332	2468	1944	1445	957	20174
Barter Is.	735	775	987	1482	1944	2337	2536	2369	2477	1923	1373	924	19862
Bethel	319	394	612	1042	1434	1866	1903	1590	1655	1173	806	402	13196
Cold Bay	474	425	525	772	918	1122	1153	1036	1122	951	791	591	9880
Cordova	366	391	522	781	1017	1221	1299	1086	1113	864	660	444	9764
Fairbanks	171	332	642	1203	1833	2254	2359	1901	1739	1068	555	222	14279
Juneau	301	338	483	725	921	1135	1237	1070	1073	810	601	381	9075
King Salmon	313	322	513	908	1290	1606	1600	1333	1411	966	673	408	11343
Kotzebue	381	446	723	1249	1728	2127	2192	1932	2080	1554	1057	636	16105
McGrath	208	338	633	1184	1791	2232	2294	1817	1758	1122	648	258	14283
Nome	481	496	693	1094	1455	1820	1879	1666	1770	1314	930	573	14171
Saint Paul	605	539	612	862	963	1197	1228	1168	1265	1098	936	726	11199
Shemya	577	475	501	784	876	1042	1045	958	1011	885	837	696	9687
Yakutat	338	347	474	716	936	1144	1169	1019	1042	840	632	435	9092
ARIZONA													
Flagstaff	46	68	201	558	867	1073	1169	991	911	651	437	180	7152
Phoenix	0	0	0	22	234	415	474	328	217	75	0	0	1765
Prescott	0	0	27	245	579	797	865	711	605	360	158	15	4362
Tucson	0	0	0	25	231	406	471	344	242	75	6	0	1800
Winslow	0	0	6	245	711	1008	1054	770	601	291	96	0	4782
Yuma	0	0	0	0	148	319	363	228	130	29	0	0	1217
ARKANSAS													
Fort Smith	0	0	12	127	450	704	781	596	456	144	22	0	3292
Little Rock	0	0	9	127	465	716	756	577	434	126	9	0	3219
Texarkana	0	0	0	78	345	561	626	468	350	105	0	0	2533
CALIFORNIA													
Bakersfield	0	0	0	37	282	502	546	364	267	105	19	0	2122
Bishop	0	0	42	248	576	797	874	666	539	306	143	36	4227
Blue Canyon	34	50	120	347	579	766	865	781	791	582	397	195	5507
Burbank	0	0	6	43	177	301	366	277	239	138	81	18	1646
Eureka	270	257	258	329	414	499	546	470	505	438	372	285	4643
Fresno	0	0	0	78	339	558	586	406	319	150	56	0	2492

Source: *Buying Solar*, Federal Energy Administration in cooperation with the Office of Consumer Affairs of the Department of Health, Education, and Welfare, June, 1976.

Table 2-1
Average Degree Days (Base 65°) (*Continued*)

State and Station	July	Aug.	Sep.	Oct.	Nov.	Dec.	Jan.	Feb.	Mar.	Apr.	May	June	Annual
Long Beach	0	0	12	40	156	288	375	297	267	168	90	18	1711
Los Angeles	28	22	42	78	180	291	372	302	288	219	158	81	2061
Mt. Shasta	25	34	123	406	696	902	983	784	738	525	347	159	5722
Oakland	53	50	45	127	309	481	527	400	353	255	180	90	2870
Point Arguello	202	186	162	205	291	400	474	392	403	339	298	243	3595
Red Bluff	0	0	0	53	318	555	605	428	341	168	47	0	2515
Sacramento	0	0	12	81	363	577	614	442	360	216	102	6	2773
Sandberg	0	0	30	202	480	691	778	661	620	426	264	57	4209
San Diego	6	0	15	37	123	251	313	249	202	123	84	36	1439
San Francisco	81	78	60	143	306	462	508	395	363	279	214	126	3015
Santa Catalina	16	0	9	50	165	279	353	308	326	249	192	105	2052
Santa Maria	99	93	96	146	270	391	459	370	363	282	233	165	2967
COLORADO													
Alamosa	65	99	279	639	1065	1420	1476	1162	1020	696	440	168	8529
Colorado Springs	9	25	132	456	825	1032	1128	938	893	582	319	84	6423
Denver	6	9	117	428	819	1035	1132	938	887	558	288	66	6283
Grand Junction	0	0	30	313	786	1113	1209	907	729	387	146	21	5641
Pueblo	0	0	54	326	750	986	1085	871	772	429	174	15	5462
CONNECTICUT													
Bridgeport	0	0	66	307	615	986	1079	966	853	510	208	27	5617
Hartford	0	6	99	372	711	1119	1209	1061	899	495	177	24	6172
New Haven	0	12	87	347	648	1011	1097	991	871	543	245	45	5897
DELAWARE													
Wilmington	0	0	51	270	588	927	980	874	735	387	112	6	4930
FLORIDA													
Apalachicola	0	0	0	16	153	319	347	260	180	33	0	0	1308
Daytona Beach	0	0	0	0	75	211	248	190	140	15	0	0	879
Fort Myers	0	0	0	0	24	109	146	101	62	0	0	0	442
Jacksonville	0	0	0	12	144	310	332	246	174	21	0	0	1239
Key West	0	0	0	0	0	28	40	31	9	0	0	0	108
Lakeland	0	0	0	0	57	164	195	146	99	0	0	0	661
Miami Beach	0	0	0	0	0	40	56	36	9	0	0	0	141
Orlando	0	0	0	0	72	198	220	165	105	6	0	0	766
Pensacola	0	0	0	19	195	353	400	277	183	36	0	0	1463
Tallahassee	0	0	0	28	198	360	375	286	202	36	0	0	1485
Tampa	0	0	0	0	60	171	202	148	102	0	0	0	683
West Palm Beach	0	0	0	0	6	65	87	64	31	0	0	0	253
GEORGIA													
Athens	0	0	12	115	405	632	642	529	431	141	22	0	2929
Atlanta	0	0	18	127	414	626	639	529	437	168	25	0	2983
Augusta	0	0	0	78	333	552	549	445	350	90	0	0	2397
Columbus	0	0	0	87	333	543	552	434	338	96	0	0	2383

Table 2-1
Average Degree Days (Base 65°) (*Continued*)

State and Station	July	Aug.	Sep.	Oct.	Nov.	Dec.	Jan.	Feb.	Mar.	Apr.	May	June	Annual
Macon	0	0	0	71	297	502	505	403	295	63	0	0	2136
Rome	0	0	24	161	474	701	710	577	468	177	34	0	3326
Savannah	0	0	0	47	246	437	437	353	254	45	0	0	1819
Thomasville	0	0	0	25	198	366	394	305	208	33	0	0	1529
IDAHO													
Boise	0	0	132	415	792	1017	1113	854	722	438	245	81	5809
Idaho Falls 46W	16	34	270	623	1056	1370	1538	1249	1085	651	391	192	8475
Idaho Falls 42NW	16	40	282	648	1107	1432	1600	1291	1107	657	388	192	8760
Lewiston	0	0	123	403	756	933	1063	815	694	426	239	90	5542
Pocatello	0	0	172	493	900	1166	1324	1058	905	555	319	141	7033
ILLINOIS													
Cairo	0	0	36	164	513	791	856	680	539	195	47	0	3821
Chicago	0	0	81	326	753	1113	1209	1044	890	480	211	48	6155
Moline	0	9	99	335	774	1181	1314	1100	918	450	189	39	6408
Peoria	0	6	87	326	759	1113	1218	1025	849	426	183	33	6025
Rockford	6	9	114	400	837	1221	1333	1137	961	516	236	60	6830
Springfield	0	0	72	291	696	1023	1135	935	769	354	136	18	5429
INDIANA													
Evansville	0	0	66	220	606	896	955	767	620	237	68	0	4435
Fort Wayne	0	9	105	378	783	1135	1178	1028	890	471	189	39	6205
Indianapolis	0	0	90	316	723	1051	1113	949	809	432	177	39	5699
South Bend	0	6	111	372	777	1125	1221	1070	933	525	239	60	6439
IOWA													
Burlington	0	0	93	322	768	1135	1259	1042	859	426	177	33	6114
Des Moines	0	9	99	363	837	1231	1398	1163	967	489	211	39	6808
Dubuque	12	31	156	450	906	1287	1420	1204	1026	546	260	78	7376
Sioux City	0	9	108	369	867	1240	1435	1198	989	483	214	39	6951
Waterloo	12	19	138	428	909	1296	1460	1221	1023	531	229	54	7320
KANSAS													
Concordia	0	0	57	276	705	1023	1163	935	781	372	149	18	5479
Dodge City	0	0	33	251	666	939	1051	840	719	354	124	9	4986
Goodland	0	6	81	381	810	1073	1166	955	884	507	236	42	6141
Topeka	0	0	57	270	672	980	1122	893	722	330	124	12	5182
Wichita	0	0	33	229	618	905	1023	804	645	270	87	6	4620
KENTUCKY													
Covington	0	0	75	291	669	983	1035	893	756	390	149	24	5265
Lexington	0	0	54	239	609	902	946	818	685	325	105	0	4683
Louisville	0	0	54	248	609	890	930	818	682	315	105	9	4660
LOUISIANA													
Alexandria	0	0	0	56	273	431	471	361	260	69	0	0	1921
Baton Rouge	0	0	0	31	216	369	409	294	208	33	0	0	1560
Burrwood	0	0	0	0	96	214	298	218	171	27	0	0	1024
Lake Charles	0	0	0	19	210	341	381	274	195	39	0	0	1459

Table 2-1

Average Degree Days (Base 65°) (*Continued*)

State and Station	July	Aug.	Sep.	Oct.	Nov.	Dec.	Jan.	Feb.	Mar.	Apr.	May	June	Annual
New Orleans	0	0	0	19	192	322	363	258	192	39	0	0	1385
Shreveport	0	0	0	47	297	477	552	426	304	81	0	0	2184
MAINE													
Caribou	78	115	336	682	1044	1535	1690	1470	1308	858	468	183	9767
Portland	12	53	195	508	807	1215	1339	1182	1042	675	372	111	7511
MARYLAND													
Baltimore	0	0	48	264	585	905	936	820	679	327	90	0	4654
Frederick	0	0	66	307	624	955	995	876	741	384	127	12	5087
MASSACHUSETTS													
Blue Hill Obsy.	0	22	108	381	690	1085	1178	1053	936	579	267	69	6368
Boston	0	9	60	316	603	983	1088	972	846	513	208	36	5634
Nantucket	12	22	93	332	573	896	992	941	896	621	384	129	5891
Pittsfield	25	59	219	524	831	1231	1339	1196	1063	660	326	105	7578
Worcester	6	34	147	450	774	1172	1271	1123	998	612	304	78	6969
MICHIGAN													
Alpena	68	105	273	580	912	1268	1404	1299	1218	777	446	156	8506
Detroit (City)	0	0	87	360	738	1088	1181	1058	936	522	220	42	6232
Escanaba	59	87	243	539	924	1293	1445	1296	1203	777	456	159	8481
Flint	16	40	159	465	843	1212	1330	1198	1066	639	319	90	7377
Grand Rapids	9	28	135	434	804	1147	1259	1134	1011	579	279	75	6894
Lansing	6	22	138	431	813	1163	1262	1142	1011	579	273	69	6909
Marquette	59	81	240	527	936	1268	1411	1268	1187	771	468	177	8393
Muskegon	12	28	120	400	762	1088	1209	1100	995	594	310	78	6696
Sault Ste. Marie	96	105	279	580	951	1367	1525	1380	1277	810	477	201	9048
MINNESOTA													
Duluth	71	109	330	632	1131	1581	1745	1518	1355	840	490	198	10000
Int Falls	71	112	363	701	1236	1724	1919	1621	1414	828	443	174	10606
Minneapolis	22	31	189	505	1014	1454	1631	1380	1166	621	288	81	8382
Rochester	25	34	186	474	1005	1438	1593	1366	1150	630	301	93	8295
Saint Cloud	28	47	225	549	1065	1500	1702	1445	1221	666	326	105	8879
MISSISSIPPI													
Jackson	0	0	0	65	315	502	546	414	310	87	0	0	2239
Meridian	0	0	0	81	339	518	543	417	310	81	0	0	2289
Vicksburg	0	0	0	53	279	462	512	384	282	69	0	0	2041
MISSOURI													
Columbia	0	0	54	251	651	967	1076	874	716	324	121	12	5046
Kansas	0	0	39	220	612	905	1032	818	682	294	109	0	4711
St. Joseph	0	6	60	285	708	1039	1172	949	769	348	133	15	5484
St. Louis	0	0	60	251	627	936	1026	848	704	312	121	15	4900
Springfield	0	0	45	223	600	877	973	781	660	291	105	6	4561
MONTANA													
Billings	6	15	186	487	897	1135	1296	1100	970	570	285	102	7049
Glasgow	31	47	270	608	1104	1466	1711	1439	1187	648	335	150	8996

Table 2-1
Average Degree Days (Base 65°) (*Continued*)

State and Station	July	Aug.	Sep.	Oct.	Nov.	Dec.	Jan.	Feb.	Mar.	Apr.	May	June	Annual
Great Falls	28	53	258	543	921	1169	1349	1154	1063	642	384	186	7750
Havre	28	53	306	595	1065	1367	1584	1364	1181	657	338	162	8700
Helena	31	59	294	601	1002	1265	1438	1170	1042	651	381	195	8129
Kalispell	50	99	321	654	1020	1240	1401	1134	1029	639	397	207	8191
Miles City	6	6	174	502	972	1296	1504	1252	1057	579	276	99	7723
Missoula	34	74	303	651	1035	1287	1420	1120	970	621	391	219	8125
NEBRASKA													
Grand Island	0	6	108	381	834	1172	1314	1089	908	462	211	45	6530
Lincoln	0	6	75	301	726	1066	1237	1016	834	402	171	30	5864
Norfolk	9	0	111	397	873	1234	1414	1179	983	498	233	48	6979
North Platte	0	6	123	440	885	1166	1271	1039	930	519	248	57	6684
Omaha	0	12	105	357	828	1175	1355	1126	939	465	208	42	6612
Scottsbluff	0	0	138	459	876	1128	1231	1008	921	552	285	75	6673
Valentine	9	12	165	493	942	1237	1395	1176	1045	579	288	84	7425
NEVADA													
Elko	9	34	225	561	924	1197	1314	1036	911	621	409	192	7433
Ely	28	43	234	592	939	1184	1308	1075	977	672	456	225	7733
Las Vegas	0	0	0	78	387	617	688	487	335	111	6	0	2709
Reno	43	87	204	490	801	1026	1073	823	729	510	357	189	6332
Winnemucca	0	34	210	536	876	1091	1172	916	837	573	363	153	6761
NEW HAMPSHIRE													
Concord	6	50	177	505	822	1240	1358	1184	1032	636	298	75	7383
Mt. Wash. Obsy.	493	536	720	1057	1341	1742	1820	1663	1652	1260	930	603	13817
NEW JERSEY													
Atlantic City	0	0	39	251	549	880	936	848	741	420	133	15	4812
Newark	0	0	30	248	573	921	983	876	729	381	118	0	4859
Trenton	0	0	57	264	576	924	989	885	753	399	121	12	4980
NEW MEXICO													
Albuquerque	0	0	12	229	642	868	930	703	595	288	81	0	4348
Clayton	0	6	66	310	699	899	986	812	747	429	183	21	5158
Raton	9	28	126	431	825	1048	1116	904	834	543	301	63	6228
Roswell	0	0	18	202	573	806	840	641	481	201	31	0	3793
Silver City	0	0	6	183	525	729	791	605	518	261	87	0	3705
NEW YORK													
Albany	0	19	138	440	777	1194	1311	1156	992	564	239	45	6875
Binghamton (AP)	22	65	201	471	810	1184	1277	1154	1045	645	313	99	7286
Binghamton (PO)	0	28	141	406	732	1107	1190	1081	949	543	229	45	6451
Buffalo	19	37	141	440	777	1156	1256	1145	1039	645	329	78	7062
Central Park	0	0	30	233	540	902	986	885	760	408	118	9	4871
J. F. Kennedy Intl	0	0	36	248	564	933	1029	935	815	480	167	12	5219
LaGuardia	0	0	27	223	528	887	973	879	750	414	124	6	4811

Table 2-1
Average Degree Days (Base 65°) (*Continued*)

State and Station	July	Aug.	Sep.	Oct.	Nov.	Dec.	Jan.	Feb.	Mar.	Apr.	May	June	Annual
Rochester	9	31	126	415	747	1125	1234	1123	1014	597	279	48	6748
Schenectady	0	22	123	422	756	1159	1283	1131	970	543	211	30	6650
Syracuse	6	28	132	415	744	1153	1271	1140	1004	570	248	45	6756
NORTH CAROLINA													
Asheville	0	0	48	245	555	775	784	683	592	273	87	0	4042
Cape Hatteras	0	0	0	78	273	521	580	518	440	177	25	0	2612
Charlotte	0	0	6	124	438	691	691	582	481	156	22	0	3191
Greensboro	0	0	33	192	513	778	784	672	552	234	47	0	3805
Raleigh	0	0	21	164	450	716	725	616	487	180	34	0	3393
Wilmington	0	0	0	74	291	521	546	462	357	96	0	0	2347
Winston Salem	0	0	21	171	483	747	753	642	524	207	37	0	3595
NORTH DAKOTA													
Bismarck	34	28	222	577	1083	1463	1708	1442	1203	645	329	117	8851
Devils Lake	40	53	273	642	1191	1634	1872	1579	1345	753	381	138	9901
Fargo	28	37	219	574	1107	1569	1789	1520	1262	690	332	99	9226
Williston	31	43	261	601	1122	1513	1758	1473	1262	681	357	141	9243
OHIO													
Akron	0	9	96	381	726	1070	1138	1016	871	489	202	39	6037
Cincinnati	0	0	54	248	612	921	970	837	701	336	118	9	4806
Cleveland	9	25	105	384	738	1088	1159	1047	918	552	260	66	6351
Columbus	0	6	84	347	714	1039	1088	949	809	426	171	27	5660
Dayton	0	6	78	310	696	1045	1097	955	809	429	167	30	5622
Mansfield	9	22	114	397	768	1110	1169	1042	924	543	245	60	6403
Sandusky	0	6	66	313	684	1032	1107	991	868	495	198	36	5796
Toledo	0	16	117	406	792	1138	1200	1056	924	543	242	60	6494
Youngstown	6	19	120	412	771	1104	1169	1047	921	540	248	60	6417
OKLAHOMA													
Oklahoma City	0	0	15	164	498	766	868	664	527	189	34	0	3725
Tulsa	0	0	18	158	522	787	893	683	539	213	47	0	3860
OREGON													
Astoria	146	130	210	375	561	679	753	622	636	480	363	231	5186
Burns	12	37	210	515	867	1113	1246	988	856	570	366	177	6957
Eugene	34	34	129	366	585	719	803	627	589	426	279	135	4726
Meacham	84	124	288	580	918	1091	1209	1005	983	726	527	339	7874
Medford	0	0	78	372	678	871	918	697	642	432	242	78	5008
Pendleton	0	0	111	350	711	884	1017	773	617	396	205	63	5127
Portland	25	28	114	335	597	735	825	644	586	396	245	105	4635
Roseburg	22	16	105	329	567	713	766	608	570	405	267	123	4491
Salem	37	31	111	338	594	729	822	647	611	417	273	144	4754
Sexton Summit	81	81	171	443	666	874	958	809	818	609	465	279	6254
PENNSYLVANIA													
Allentown	0	0	90	353	693	1045	1116	1002	849	471	167	24	5810
Erie	0	25	102	391	714	1063	1169	1081	973	585	288	60	6451

Table 2-1
Average Degree Days (Base 65°) (*Continued*)

State and Station	July	Aug.	Sep.	Oct.	Nov.	Dec.	Jan.	Feb.	Mar.	Apr.	May	June	Annual
Harrisburg	0	0	63	298	648	992	1045	907	766	396	124	12	5251
Philadelphia	0	0	60	291	621	964	1014	890	744	390	115	12	5101
Pittsburgh	0	9	105	375	726	1063	1119	1002	874	480	195	39	5987
Reading	0	0	54	257	597	939	1001	885	735	372	105	0	4945
Scranton	0	19	132	434	762	1104	1156	1028	893	498	195	33	6254
Williamsport	0	9	111	375	717	1073	1122	1002	856	468	177	24	5934
RHODE ISLAND													
Block Is.	0	16	78	307	594	902	1020	955	877	612	344	99	5804
Providence	0	16	96	372	660	1023	1110	988	868	534	236	51	5954
SOUTH CAROLINA													
Charleston	0	0	0	59	282	471	487	389	291	54	0	0	2033
Columbia	0	0	0	84	345	577	570	470	357	81	0	0	2484
Florence	0	0	0	78	315	552	552	459	347	84	0	0	2387
Greenville	0	0	0	112	387	636	648	535	434	120	12	0	2884
Spartanburg	0	0	15	130	417	667	663	560	453	144	25	0	3074
SOUTH DAKOTA													
Huron	9	12	165	508	1014	1432	1628	1355	1125	600	288	87	8223
Rapid City	22	12	165	481	897	1172	1333	1145	1051	615	326	126	7345
Sioux Falls	19	25	168	462	972	1361	1544	1285	1082	573	270	78	7839
TENNESSEE													
Bristol	0	0	51	236	573	828	828	700	598	261	68	0	4143
Chattanooga	0	0	18	143	468	698	722	577	453	150	25	0	3254
Knoxville	0	0	30	171	489	725	732	613	493	198	43	0	3494
Memphis	0	0	18	130	447	698	729	585	456	147	22	0	3232
Nashville	0	0	30	158	495	732	778	644	512	189	40	0	3578
Oak Ridge (CO)	0	0	39	192	531	772	778	669	552	228	56	0	3817
TEXAS													
Abilene	0	0	0	99	366	586	642	470	347	114	0	0	2624
Amarillo	0	0	18	205	570	797	877	664	546	252	56	0	3985
Austin	0	0	0	31	225	388	468	325	223	51	0	0	1711
Brownsville	0	0	0	0	66	149	205	106	74	0	0	0	600
Corpus Christi	0	0	0	0	120	220	291	174	109	0	0	0	914
Dallas	0	0	0	62	321	524	601	440	319	90	6	0	2363
El Paso	0	0	0	84	414	648	685	445	319	105	0	0	2700
Fort Worth	0	0	0	65	324	536	614	448	319	99	0	0	2405
Galveston	0	0	0	0	138	270	350	258	189	30	0	0	1235
Houston	0	0	0	6	183	307	384	288	192	36	0	0	1396
Laredo	0	0	0	0	105	217	267	134	74	0	0	0	797
Lubbock	0	0	18	174	513	744	800	613	484	201	31	0	3578
Midland	0	0	0	87	381	592	651	468	322	90	0	0	2591
Port Arthur	0	0	0	22	207	329	384	274	192	39	0	0	1447
San Angelo	0	0	0	68	318	536	567	412	288	66	0	0	2255
San Antonio	0	0	0	31	207	363	428	286	195	39	0	0	1549

Table 2-1

Average Degree Days (Base 65°) (*Continued*)

State and Station	July	Aug.	Sep.	Oct.	Nov.	Dec.	Jan.	Feb.	Mar.	Apr.	May	June	Annual
Victoria	0	0	0	6	150	270	344	230	152	21	0	0	1173
Waco	0	0	0	43	270	456	536	389	270	66	0	0	2030
Wichita Falls	0	0	0	99	381	632	698	518	378	120	6	0	2832
UTAH													
Milford	0	0	99	443	867	1141	1252	988	822	519	279	87	6497
Salt Lake City	0	0	81	419	849	1082	1172	910	763	459	233	84	6052
Wendover	0	0	48	372	822	1091	1178	902	729	408	177	51	5778
VERMONT													
Burlington	28	65	207	539	891	1349	1513	1333	1187	714	353	90	8269
VIRGINIA													
Cape Henry	0	0	0	112	360	645	694	633	536	246	53	0	3279
Lynchburg	0	0	51	223	540	822	849	731	605	267	78	0	4166
Norfolk	0	0	0	136	408	698	738	655	533	216	37	0	3421
Richmond	0	0	36	214	495	784	815	703	546	219	53	0	3865
Roanoke	0	0	51	229	549	825	834	722	614	261	65	0	4150
Wash. Nat'l. Ap.	0	0	33	217	519	834	871	762	626	288	74	0	4224
WASHINGTON													
Olympia	68	71	198	422	636	753	834	675	645	450	307	177	5236
Seattle	50	47	129	329	543	657	738	599	577	396	242	117	4424
Seattle Boeing	34	40	147	384	624	763	831	655	608	411	242	99	4838
Seattle Tacoma	56	62	162	391	633	750	828	678	657	474	295	159	5145
Spokane	9	25	168	493	879	1082	1231	980	834	531	288	135	6655
Stampede Pass	273	291	393	701	1008	1178	1287	1075	1085	855	654	483	9283
Tatoosh Is.	295	279	306	406	534	639	713	613	645	525	431	333	5719
Walla Walla	0	0	87	310	681	843	986	745	589	342	177	45	4805
Yakima	0	12	144	450	828	1039	1163	868	713	435	220	69	5941
WEST VIRGINIA													
Charleston	0	0	63	254	591	865	880	770	648	300	96	9	4476
Elkins	9	25	135	400	729	992	1008	896	791	444	198	48	5675
Huntington	0	0	63	257	585	856	880	764	636	294	99	12	4446
Parkersburg	0	0	60	264	606	905	942	826	691	339	115	6	4754
WISCONSIN													
Green Bay	28	50	174	484	924	1333	1494	1313	1141	654	335	99	8029
La Crosse	12	19	153	437	924	1339	1504	1277	1070	540	245	69	7589
Madison	25	40	174	474	930	1330	1473	1274	1113	618	310	102	7863
Milwaukee	43	47	174	471	876	1252	1376	1193	1054	642	372	135	7635
WYOMING													
Casper	6	16	192	524	942	1169	1290	1084	1020	657	381	129	7410
Cheyenne	19	31	210	543	924	1101	1228	1056	1011	672	381	102	7278
Lander	6	19	204	555	1020	1299	1417	1145	1017	654	381	153	7870
Sheridan	25	31	219	539	948	1200	1355	1154	1054	642	366	150	7683

Infiltration Heat Loss

Let's explore the window-door infiltration formula in Energy Work Sheet 4 by first looking at its little brother:

(Equation 3)

$$H_{in} = C \times L \times Q \times (T_i - T_0)$$

where H_{in} = heat loss per hour by infiltration through door or window (Btuh)

C = heat capacity of air (0.018 Btu/cubic foot/°F)

L = total crack length (feet)

Q = rate of air leakage (cubic feet/hour/foot of crack)

$(T_i - T_0)$ = temperature difference between indoor and outdoor air (°F)

According to Equation 3, hourly infiltration heat loss from a door or window depends on four factors. You've probably already measured your L's (crack lengths), and you understand $(T_i - T_0)$ because you encountered it in Equation 1. But what of C and Q? Well, C is a constant, a measure of air's ability to absorb heat. And here Q represents the amount of air that can leak hourly through each linear foot of window or door crack. As you might expect, Q varies according to wind velocity and general window or door condition (type of construction, frame-to-sash (-door) fit, weatherstripping, etc.). So where do you turn when you want the Q-value for one of your windows or doors? You turn to Table 2-2, which gives you Q for window and door types in different conditions under various wind speeds. The trick is to match as closely as possible your own doors or windows to those described on the chart, select appropriate wind velocities, and read the corresponding values of Q.

Let's say you want an estimate of how much heat you're losing through the cracks on one of your 3-x-5-foot double-hung nonweatherstripped wood windows. And suppose you have an indoor/outdoor temperature difference of 60°F and a 10 mph wind pushing against the house. According to Table 2-2, the rate of air leakage (Q) around such a window in a 10 mph zephyr is 21 cubic feet/hour/foot of crack. So your estimated heat loss per hour due to infiltration is:

$$H_{in} = 0.018 \times 19 \times 21 \times 60 = 431 \text{ Btuh}$$

That's 10,344 Btu per day. At that rate, your nonweatherstripped window could lose $10 to $20 worth of fuel per heating season. If all your windows

Table 2-2
Air Leakage (Q) for Windows and Doors

Window or Door Type	Q (cu. ft./ft. of crack/hr.) Wind Speed (mph)					
	5	10	15	20	25	30
Double-hung, wood sash[1]						
Average fit, not weatherstripped	7	21	39	59	80	104
Average fit, weatherstripped	4	13	24	36	49	63
Poor fit, not weatherstripped	27	69	111	154	199	249
Poor fit, weatherstripped	6	19	34	51	71	92
Poor fit, not weatherstripped, with storm sash	14	35	56	77	100	125
Double-hung, metal sash						
Not weatherstripped	20	47	74	104	137	170
Weatherstripped	6	19	32	46	60	76
Rolled section, steel sash, residential casement						
$\frac{1}{64}$-inch sash-to-frame gap	6	18	33	47	60	74
$\frac{1}{32}$-inch sash-to-frame gap	14	32	52	76	100	128
Hollow metal, vertically pivoted sash	30	88	145	186	221	242
Residential door						
Good fit	27	69	111	154	199	249
Poor fit	54	138	222	308	398	498
Good fit, weatherstripped	14	35	56	77	100	125
Poor fit, weatherstripped	27	69	111	154	199	249

[1]An average fitted double-hung wood window has a $\frac{1}{16}$-inch gap between sash and frame *and* a $\frac{3}{64}$-inch difference between window frame guide and sash thickness. A poorly fitted specimen is much looser— $\frac{3}{32}$ inch between sash perimeter and frame and $\frac{3}{32}$-inch difference between frame guide and sash thickness.

were in that sad shape, you'd be royally fleeced every winter. All because of a few crevices.

Naturally, Equation 3 is not the formula to use if you want window-door infiltration loss estimates for a whole year. For that we need an equation that takes into account year-round temperature fluctuations. The formula that does this is the one on your Work Sheet, namely Equation 3 with $(T_i - T_0)$ replaced by 24 hours $\times$ D:

(Equation 4)

$$H_{in} = C \times L \times Q \times 24 \text{ hours} \times D$$

where H_{in} now equals heat lost per year by infiltration through door or window (Btu), and we've seen all the other symbols before. But what wind speed value do you use here to find Q? Since Equation 4 spits out *annual* heat loss numbers, you should plug in average *annual* wind speed data. And you'll find that data in Table 2-3. Once you know what the average wind speed is for your area, round it off to the nearest wind speed in Table 2-2 and extract Q.

Now let's give Equation 4 a try. Suppose you live in Youngstown, Ohio. That means you have 6417 degree days each year (Table 2-1) and an average yearly wind speed of about 10 mph (Table 2-3). Given those parameters, the estimated annual infiltration loss of that drafty window we were discussing would be:

$$H_{in} = 0.018 \times 19 \times 21 \times 24 \times 6417 = 1,106,085 \text{ Btu, or } 1.10 \text{ million Btu}$$

If you're paying $12 per million Btu of fuel (and you very well may be), 1.10 million Btu would cost you $13.20.

Now you know how to figure the annual infiltration heat loss for every window and outer door you have. Add up all those losses and you'll get an estimate of your total window-door infiltration loss per heating season.

But let's not forget about infiltration loss through exterior walls. Wall infiltration is usually less of a problem than window-door infiltration, but it is often serious enough to worry about and to quantify. Unless your sidewalls are sealed with vapor barriers and seamless plaster (and consequently have negligible infiltration, not worth computing), you'd be smart to figure out the Btu's those walls leak away.

If you can compute your air seepage heat losses through windows and doors, calculating your sidewall infiltration losses will be a cinch. Take a look at the infiltration formula from Work Sheet 2:

(Equation 5)

$$H_{in} = C \times S \times Q \times 24 \text{ hours} \times D$$

It's nearly identical to Equation 4; the only difference is that S has replaced L. The reason is that Q-values for an exterior wall are expressed in cubic feet/hour/*square foot of wall area* (see Table 2-4), unlike Q-values for windows and doors which are in cubic feet/hour/*foot of crack*. For Equation 4, you measure crack length in feet, L; for Equation 5 you measure wall area in square feet, S. Otherwise, everything you learned about solving Equation 4 applies to solving Equation 5. Just keep your L's and S's straight—and, of course, record your total yearly wall infiltration loss on the Work Sheet. (See sample calculation in Figure 2-1.)

Table 2-3

Average Yearly Wind Speed for Selected Cities

State and Station	Average Wind Speed (mph)	State and Station	Average Wind Speed (mph)	State and Station	Average Wind Speed (mph)
ALABAMA		**GEORGIA**		**MASSACHUSETTS**	
Birmingham	7.9	Atlanta	9.7	Boston	13.3
Mobile	10.0	Augusta	6.3		
Montgomery	6.9	Macon	8.9	**MICHIGAN**	
ALASKA		Savannah	8.4	Detroit (City AP)	10.3
				Flint	9.0
Anchorage	6.8	**HAWAII**		Grand Rapids	9.8
Cold Bay	17.4	Hilo	8.7		
Fairbanks	5.2	Honolulu	12.1	**MINNESOTA**	
King Salmon	11.4			Duluth	12.6
ARIZONA		**IDAHO**		Minneapolis	11.2
Phoenix	5.4	Boise	8.9	**MISSISSIPPI**	
Tucson	8.1	**ILLINOIS**		Jackson	7.1
		Chicago (O'Hare)	11.2		
ARKANSAS		Chicago (Midway)	10.2	**MISSOURI**	
Little Rock	8.7	Moline	10.0	Kansas City	9.8
		Springfield	12.0	St. Louis	9.3
CALIFORNIA				Springfield	12.9
Bakersfield	5.8	**INDIANA**			
Burbank	4.5	Evansville	9.1	**MONTANA**	
Fresno	6.1	Fort Wayne	10.9	Great Falls	13.9
Los Angeles	6.8	Indianapolis	10.8		
Oakland	7.5	South Bend	10.9	**NEBRASKA**	
Sacramento	9.3			Omaha	11.6
San Diego	6.3	**IOWA**			
San Francisco	10.6	Des Moines	12.1	**NEVADA**	
		Sioux City	11.7	Las Vegas	9.7
COLORADO				Reno	5.9
Colorado Springs	10.0	**KANSAS**			
Denver	10.0	Topeka	11.2	**NEW JERSEY**	
		Wichita	13.7	Newark	9.8
CONNECTICUT					
Hartford	9.8	**KENTUCKY**		**NEW MEXICO**	
DISTRICT OF COLUMBIA		Lexington	10.1	Albuquerque	8.6
Washington	9.7	Louisville	8.8		
				NEW YORK	
DELAWARE		**LOUISIANA**		Albany	8.6
Wilmington	8.8	Baton Rouge	8.3	Binghamton	10.0
		Lake Charles	8.5	Buffalo	12.4
FLORIDA		New Orleans	9.0	New York	12.0
Jacksonville	8.9	Shreveport	9.5	(Kennedy)	
Miami	8.8			New York (La	12.9
Orlando	8.6	**MAINE**		Guardia)	
Tallahassee	6.1	Portland	9.6	Rochester	11.2
Tampa	8.8			Syracuse	9.7
West Palm Beach	10.5	**MARYLAND**			
		Baltimore	10.4		

Table 2-3
Average Yearly Wind Speed for Selected Cities (*Continued*)

State and Station	Average Wind Speed (mph)	State and Station	Average Wind Speed (mph)	State and Station	Average Wind Speed (mph)
NORTH CAROLINA		**RHODE ISLAND**		**UTAH**	
Charlotte	7.9	Providence	10.7	Salt Lake City	8.7
Greensboro	8.0	**SOUTH CAROLINA**		**VERMONT**	
Raleigh	7.7	Charleston	9.2	Burlington	8.3
Winston-Salem	9.0	Columbia	7.0		
NORTH DAKOTA		**SOUTH DAKOTA**		**VIRGINIA**	
Bismarck	11.2	Huron	11.9	Norfolk	10.2
Fargo	14.4	Rapid City	11.0	Richmond	7.8
				Roanoke	8.3
OHIO		**TENNESSEE**		**WASHINGTON**	
Akron-Canton	10.4	Chattanooga	6.1		
Cincinnati	9.6	Knoxville	7.5	Seattle-Tacoma AP	10.7
Cleveland	11.6	Memphis	9.4		
Columbus	8.2	Nashville	7.2	Spokane	8.1
Dayton	10.3	**TEXAS**		**WEST VIRGINIA**	
Youngstown	10.3	Amarillo	12.9	Charleston	6.2
OKLAHOMA		Austin	9.7		
Oklahoma City	14.0	Brownsville	12.3	**WISCONSIN**	
Tulsa	10.6	Corpus Christi	11.9	Green Bay	11.2
		Dallas	11.0	Madison	10.1
OREGON		El Paso	11.3	Milwaukee	12.1
Medford	4.6	Ft. Worth	12.5		
Portland	7.7	Galveston	12.5	**WYOMING**	
Salem	7.1	Houston	11.8	Casper	13.3
		Laredo	12.3		
PENNSYLVANIA		Lubbock	13.6	**PACIFIC**	
Harrisburg	7.3	Midland	10.1	Wake Island	14.6
Philadelphia	9.6	San Antonio	9.3	**PUERTO RICO**	
Pittsburgh	9.4	Waco	12.5	San Juan	9.1
Scranton	8.8	Wichita Falls	10.5		

Source: *Climatology of the United States Series 82; Decennial Census of the United States Climate: Summary of Hourly Observations, 1951–60.*

Like Equation 4, Equation 5 has a little brother that tells you *hourly* heat loss:

(Equation 6) $$H_{in} = C \times S \times Q \times (T_i - T_0)$$

And yes, once you know a barrier's annual transmission loss and annual infiltration loss, you simply add those numbers to find the complete annual barrier loss.

Energy Work Sheet 2: Exterior Walls

EXTERIOR WALL AREA

$\underline{45} \times \underline{8} = \underline{360}$ sq. ft.

$\underline{45} \times \underline{8} = \underline{360}$ sq. ft.

$\underline{35} \times \underline{8} = \underline{280}$ sq. ft.

$\underline{35} \times \underline{8} = \underline{280}$ sq. ft.

$\underline{1280}$ sq. ft. Total Exterior Wall Area

WALL U- AND R-VALUES

Material	R-Value
INDOOR AIR FILM	0.68 [1]
GYPSUM BOARD, 1/2 IN.	0.45
AIR SPACE, 4 IN.	1.21
PLYWOOD SHEATHING, 1/2 IN.	0.63
LAPPED SIDING, 1/2 x 8 IN.	0.81
OUTDOOR AIR FILM	0.17 [2]
	3.95 Total R-Value
	0.25 Total U-Value (U = 1/R)

ANNUAL TRANSMISSION HEAT LOSS

U $\times$ A $\times$ 24 hours $\times$ D = Annual Transmission Heat Loss

$\underline{0.25} \times \underline{1280} \times$ 24 hours $\times \underline{6172} = \underline{47,400,960}$ Btu

ANNUAL INFILTRATION HEAT LOSS

C $\times$ S $\times$ Q $\times$ 24 hours $\times$ D = Annual Infiltration Heat Loss

$0.018 \times \underline{1280} \times \underline{4} \times$ 24 hours $\times \underline{6172} = \underline{13,651,476}$ Btu

ANNUAL BARRIER HEAT LOSS

Annual Transmission Heat Loss + Annual Infiltration Heat Loss = Annual Barrier Heat Loss

$\underline{47,400,960} + \underline{13,651,476} = \underline{61,052,436}$ Btu

▪ ANNUAL BARRIER HEATING COSTS

Annual Barrier Heat Loss $\times$ Cost of Fuel Per Btu = Annual Barrier Heating Costs

$\underline{61,052,436} \times \$ \underline{00.000008} = \$ \underline{488.42}$

---

[1] If applicable, insert indoor air film R-value here.
[2] If applicable, insert outdoor air film R-value here.

Fig. 2-1. Sample Energy Work Sheet for an Exterior Wall. The degree day figure is for Hartford, Connecticut.

Table 2-4
Air Leakage (Q) for Exterior Walls

Wall Type	Q (cu. ft./sq. ft. of wall/hr.) Wind Speed (mph)					
	5	10	15	20	25	30
Brick wall, unplastered, 8½ inches, workmanship poor	2	4	8	12	19	23
Brick wall, unplastered, 13 inches, workmanship poor	1	4	7	12	16	21
Frame wall, unplastered	3	7	15	20	27	25

Note: Figures for other types of walls are not yet available.
Use the figure for the wall that most closely approximates the type of wall in your house.

Total Annual Heat Loss

As you know, your house loses virtually all its heat by conduction and infiltration. So your *total* annual heat loss = *total* annual transmission heat loss + *total* annual infiltration heat loss. Or, to put it another way, your overall yearly heat loss equals your annual barrier losses. Your answer to this bit of addition may be way over 100 million Btu, or it could be a lot less. But whatever your yearly loss is, you can diminish it through conservation. And when you do, the Btu-saving power of your efforts will be accurately reflected in that telltale number: total annual heat loss.

The fact is, total annual heat loss is a better yardstick of weatherization effectiveness than annual energy usage derived from your heating bills. If you compare annual usages from the bills of two consecutive years to see if your new attic insulation is doing its job, you may end up puzzled. Since the weather varies from one heating season to the next, your heating fuel requirements will vary from year to year. And you often can't tell whether a fuel savings on your heating bill is due to more weatherization or better weather. Also, the usage shown on your bills can fluctuate because of varying heating plant efficiency. If you pump 5 million Btu of fuel oil into your furnace, you'll get only about 3.75 million Btu of heat. If you're lucky. The truth is, most heating systems are not 100% efficient at converting fuel into heat. So if your furnace efficiency drops (because the unit needs cleaning, something gets out of adjustment, or whatever), your fuel usage will probably increase. And when that increase shows up on your bills, it will make your insulation look less effective.

To get a clear picture of your energy savings, look at your total annual heat loss figures. Only they permit comparison of the most important facts. They allow you to weigh not how many Btu's you buy, but how many you waste. The former is of interest; the latter is crucial, because heat loss is the thing that most affects your heating costs. And because your annual loss figures reflect perfectly average weather (temperatures and wind velocity), you can correlate them year to year. A bad winter storm won't prejudice your numbers. Your heating bill, yes, but not your numbers.

Heating Costs

Energy is money. Money is energy. That's why it's hard to talk about annual heat loss without discussing heating costs. Once you know how much energy slips out of your house, you naturally want to hear how much all that slipping costs. And a formula on your Work Sheets tells you—it translates Btu's into dollars and cents:

(Equation 7)

$$\frac{\text{Annual}}{\text{Heat Loss}} \times \frac{\text{Cost of}}{\text{Fuel per Btu}} = \frac{\text{Annual}}{\text{Heating Costs}}$$

For example, if your exterior walls have a yearly heat loss of 20 million Btu and your heating fuel costs \$0.000008 per Btu, your penalty for having such leaky walls is \$160 annually:

$$20{,}000{,}000 \text{ Btu} \times \$0.000008 \text{ per Btu} = \$160$$

And, of course, figuring your overall yearly heating costs is as simple as adding up the annual costs for all your barriers.

To find your fuel cost per Btu, simply ask your utility company or supplier. If all they can give you is cost per gallon or cost per kilowatt-hour or cost per anything except Btu's, you'll have to convert their figures. The conversion table in Table 2-5 should be a big help.

If your annual heat loss numbers reflect typical weather, then obviously so does your Work Sheet heating costs. Consequently, you shouldn't expect heating bill charges to match your calculated costs. If, however, the difference between the two seems outrageous, you can check for sources of error—bad arithmetic, sloppy inspection, a wintertime thermostat setting above 65°F (the standard for degree days), or exposed pipes and ductwork that lose heat unaccounted for in your figures.

The next section will offer positive proof that chugging through those

Table 2-5
Costs of Fuels per Quantity and per Btu

FUEL OIL

$ Per Gallon	$ Per 1000 BTU	$ Per Gallon	$ Per 1000 BTU	$ Per Gallon	$ Per 1000 BTU
.55	.0055	.95	.0095	1.35	.0135
.60	.0060	1.00	.0100	1.40	.0140
.65	.0065	1.05	.0105	1.45	.0145
.70	.0070	1.10	.0110	1.50	.0150
.75	.0075	1.15	.0115	1.55	.0155
.80	.0080	1.20	.0120	1.60	.0160
.85	.0085	1.25	.0125		
.90	.0090	1.30	.0130		

ELECTRICITY

$ Per KWH	$. Per 1000 BTU	$ Per KWH	$ Per 1000 BTU	$ Per KWH	$ Per 1000 BTU
.03	.0088	.05	.0147	.07	.0207
.035	.0103	.055	.0162	.075	.0222
.04	.0118	.06	.0177	.08	.0237
.045	.0132	.065	.0192	.085	.0252

NATURAL GAS

$ Per 1000 CU. FT.	$ Per 1000 BTU	$ Per 1000 CU. FT.	$ Per 1000 BTU	$ Per 1000 CU. FT.	$ Per 1000 BTU
2.50	.0036	3.50	.0050	4.50	.0066
2.75	.0039	3.75	.0054	4.75	.0070
3.00	.0043	4.00	.0058	5.00	.0074
3.25	.0046	4.25	.0062	5.25	.0078

Note: These figures refer to BTUs extracted from fuel at standard heating plant efficiencies.

Work Sheet cost calculations is worth the bother. For now, let's just say that because those calculated heating costs tell you the dollar value of wasted heat with the weather factor held constant, they help you make uncomplicated comparisons of different conservation options. That means if you want to know whether one weatherization scheme saves more fuel money than another, you can turn to Equation 7. It'll help you compare the most significant facts—the costs of heat losses connected with each strategy. And the weather won't sabotage your conclusions.

Design Heat Load

What if one winter night a blizzard came blasting out of the north, hurling winds that made your house tremble, pushing the mercury lower than you'd ever seen it—could your heating system keep your family warm? Answering that important question means taking a hard look at your house's *design heat load.* That's the hourly heat loss from your house under fearsome weather conditions, with the lowest expected outdoor temperature (winter design temperature) and an above-average wind speed. The word "load" reminds us that heat lost from your home in winter is a heating demand on your furnace. And, as you know, if your furnace can't continually replace the heat that slips through your barriers, Btu for Btu, your indoor temperature will drop. So your design heat load tells you what capacity your heating system *must* have to keep you warm when winter pours it on.

To determine your design heat load you just compute the hourly heat loss of each of your barriers when the weather is especially nasty, and then add up those losses. Use Equation 1 to figure your hourly transmission losses and Equations 3 and 6 to calculate your hourly infiltration losses. Factor in the bad weather by substituting your area's winter design temperature into each of those formulas *and* assuming a 15-mph wind for Equations 3 and 6. (That 15-mph wind speed is above average for most parts of the country, a reasonable figure for design load conditions.) Derive your winter design temperature from Table 2-6 (use the location nearest you) and get your indoor temp (T_i) from an objective assessment of what your thermostat (or indoor thermometer) says *most the time.*

Your calculations should lead you to that vital question, "Does my design heat load exceed (or match) my heating system capacity?" That is, can your furnace keep up with the hourly heat loss from your house under severe winter conditions? That's the bottom line. Obviously, if your design heat load is 50,000 Btuh and your furnace's capacity is only 45,000 Btuh, your house could get awfully cold awfully fast on an awfully bitter winter day. And if your design load is equal to your furnace output (or darn close), you're risking your indoor comfort. What if your furnace efficiency drops a bit? Or Old Man Winter decides to set a record for meanness? Or your design load figure represents your *minimum* hourly heat loss? Better to have a heating system capacity that tops your design load by at least 10%. Ask a reputable service technician about your heating system output; you may need more capacity than you think.

Table 2-6
Winter Design Temperatures for Selected Sites

State and Station	Winter Design Temperature °F	State and Station	Winter Design Temperature °F	State and Station	Winter Design Temperature °F
ALABAMA		**ILLINOIS**		**MISSOURI**	
Birmingham	18	Chicago	−4	Columbia	4
Fairhope	28	Kankakee	−4	St. Joseph	−2
Selma	23	Springfield	−1	**MONTANA**	
ALASKA		**INDIANA**		Billings	−16
Anchorage	−25	Bloomington	3	Helena	−23
Fairbanks	−53	Gary	−2	**NEBRASKA**	
ARIZONA		**IOWA**		Grand Island	−6
Flagstaff	0	Cedar Rapids	−7	Kearney	−10
Phoenix	31	Des Moines	−8	**NEVADA**	
ARKANSAS		**KANSAS**		Carson City	6
Camden	19	Dodge City	3	Elko	−13
Little Rock	15	Kansas City	4	**NEW HAMPSHIRE**	
CALIFORNIA		**KENTUCKY**		Concord	−8
Berkeley	37	Ashland	14	Pease AFB	−2
Fresno	27	Lexington	6	**NEW JERSEY**	
San Francisco	36	**LOUISIANA**		Atlantic City	11
COLORADO		Baton Rouge	27	Trenton	3
Denver	−3	Shreveport	21	**NEW MEXICO**	
CONNECTICUT		**MAINE**		Albuquerque	14
Bridgeport	8	Augusta	−10	Santa Fe	−4
Hartford	3	Portland	−6	**NEW YORK**	
DELAWARE		**MARYLAND**		Albany	−1
Dover AFB	13	Annapolis USNA	15	Buffalo	3
Wilmington	12	Cumberland	8	Kennedy Airport	12
DISTRICT OF COLUMBIA		**MASSACHUSETTS**		**NORTH CAROLINA**	
Washington	11	Cambridge	6	Asheville	13
		Lawrence	−5	Charlotte	18
FLORIDA		Salem	0	**NORTH DAKOTA**	
Daytona Beach	36	**MICHIGAN**		Bismarck	−25
Miami	44	Ann Arbor	−4	Fargo	−24
GEORGIA		Detroit	4	**OHIO**	
Albany	26	Marquette	−9	Canton	1
Augusta	20	**MINNESOTA**		Dayton	1
HAWAII		Duluth	−19	Toledo	0
Pearl Harbor	62	Worthington	−12	**OKLAHOMA**	
IDAHO		**MISSISSIPPI**		Enid	10
Boise	5	Biloxi	30	Tulsa	12
Twin Falls	−5	Jackson	23		

Table 2-6
Winter Design Temperatures for Selected Sites (*Continued*)

State and Station	Winter Design Temperature °F	State and Station	Winter Design Temperature °F	State and Station	Winter Design Temperature °F
OREGON		**TEXAS**		**WASHINGTON**	
Eugene	20	Abilene	17	Aberdeen	25
Portland	22	Austin	25	Richland	−4
		Fort Worth	20	Walla Walla	7
PENNSYLVANIA		Laredo AFB	33		
Allentown	8	Waco	21	**WEST VIRGINIA**	
Altoona	−5			Charleston	9
Harrisburg	10	**UTAH**		Elkins	1
York	11	Logan	−7	Wheeling	4
		Provo	2		
RHODE ISLAND				**WISCONSIN**	
Kingston	5	**VERMONT**		Beloit	−9
Providence	5	Burlington	−12	Green Bay	−12
		North Concord AFS	−21		
SOUTH CAROLINA				**WYOMING**	
Columbia	23			Casper	−11
Greenville	18	**VIRGINIA**		Cheyenne	−2
		Charlottesville	11	Sheridan	−12
SOUTH DAKOTA		Hampton	19		
Huron	−17	Roanoke	15		
Sioux Falls	−15				
TENNESSEE					
Chattanooga	17				
Nashville	12				

Source: Air Force, Army, and Navy manual, *Engineering Weather Data.*

And by the way, a fully weatherized house generally has *one third* the design heat load of an uninsulated, uncaulked one. That's a *big* difference in heating bills. Big enough to make home weatherization serious business.

FIGURING YOUR BEST WEATHERIZATION INVESTMENTS

All your inspecting and calculating leads here—to a dollars and cents evaluation of your most important weatherization options. This analysis is fueled by your Work Sheet data, takes into account all those troublesome variables discussed in chapter 1, is recorded on your Evaluation Sheets (see page 55), and answers this Big Question:

Given the limitations of your budget, what is the best combination of weatherization measures for your house?

The answer to that question contains the answers to many more—for instance, about payback periods for each weatherization measure you consider, about the strategy that offers the highest net savings, and about weatherization techniques that waste money.

Since resolving that Big Question is what this investment evaluation is all about, let's begin by looking a little closer at what's being asked. In this analysis "the best combination of weatherization measures" means the package that gives you more *net savings* than any other. Net savings is the money saved from weatherization minus the cost of that weatherization. So another way of stating the question is, "What program of weatherization investments will allow you to maximize your net savings while staying within your budget?"

The Benefit/Cost Ratio

To figure out the plan that gives you the most net savings, we need a powerful analytic tool, called the benefit/cost (or savings-to-investment) ratio. A benefit/cost ratio enables you to compare the savings you get from weatherization with the cost of weatherization. For example, if you install insulation in your attic at a cost of $500, and the stuff saves you $4,000 over the years, you have a benefit/cost ratio of $4000/$500 = 8.0. That means for every dollar invested in the insulation, there's an $8.00 return. (Would that banks were so generous.) If, on the other hand, the ratio were 1.0, you would just break even. And if the ratio were less than 1.0, you would lose money.

Now let's suppose you're mulling over a lot of weatherization tactics. And say you have $1500 to spend on them and you know the benefit/cost ratio of each one. What combination of options would save you the most money? If you were to rank all those options by benefit/cost ratio, highest to lowest, and select one at a time in descending order until the cost of your choices just about equalled $1500, you'd have your answer. You'd glean from a hoard of possibilities the *one* package of options that could give you the most net savings for a $1500 price tag. No other $1500 combination could deliver as much. And few other mathematical indices could tell you as much about your weatherization program as benefit/cost ratios.

This kind of benefit/cost analysis is quite versatile. You can use it to design any size weatherization combination you want. But such a dollar-and-cents appraisal is also static and simplified. And purposely so. It is static because it ignores inflation. And it ignores it because you can conduct a serviceable evaluation without considering rising fuel prices; they can only *increase* your weatherization savings. It is simplified because our appraisal is stripped of those money factors that probably will have minimal effect on your conclusions—e.g., cost of repairs to installations, salvage value of weatherization materials, and replacement costs. It is simplified, too, because it's designed to help us scrutinize only the big money-savers—thermal insulation, storm windows, special glazing, window "covers," and weatherstripping.

Selecting Options to Evaluate

Here are some guidelines for choosing options to put to the test.

1. For each barrier or weatherization problem you suspect needs attention, first propose a "standard" solution. That is, enter on the proper Evaluation Sheet the feasible option recommended by the experts. Regardless of whether you can afford such an option, it will give you a point of reference, a ratio to compare with other ratios. And you might discover that the recommended cure is not as cost-effective as another.

Here is what the experts recommend. For minimum standard insulation levels for exterior walls, for floors over an unheated space, and for ceilings, attics, or roofs, see Figure 2-2. FHA minimum property standards require storm or double-glazed windows in areas with more than 4500 annual degree days; windows and doors in areas with fewer degree days should at least be weatherstripped. Usually, crawl space barriers in regions with a winter design temperature of 10°F or less should get perimeter insulation with an R-value of at least 6.0. Most basement wall barriers require insulation worth at least an R-value of 7.0, and especially cold areas may demand even more. (However, in far northern reaches like Alaska and Minnesota, and deep southern areas like Texas and Florida, there should be *no* basement barrier insulation. See chapter 3 for details.) Slab barriers deserve at least an inch of rigid perimeter insulation.

Note that I said to enter the recommended *feasible* option. That's the one that comes closest to what the experts want while allowing for any construction limitations of your house. You'll find discussion of those limitations and other feasibility factors in the next three chapters.

2. For each barrier or problem that needs fixing, propose a "minimal" option, one that affords you only a fraction of the heat-retarding power you'd like. Examining such schemes will tell you a lot about the economics

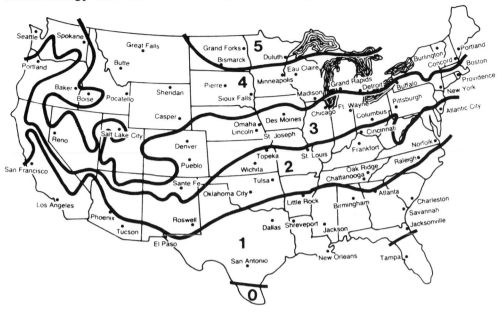

Zone	FHA-Recommended R-Value Ceiling/Roof/Attic	Wall	Floor
0,1	26	13	11
2	26	19	13
3	30	19	19
4	33	19	22
5	38	19	22

Fig. 2-2. FHA Recommended Insulation Levels.

of *not* spending a lot of weatherization dollars, and it will give you a point of reference for comparing other options. Who knows, perhaps a cheapie will turn out to be a better investment than any other option you consider. Remember, though, you may need to beef up small increments of weatherization later on.

3. Propose one or two mid-range weatherization options, ones that have more Btu-saving power than the minimal options and less than the recommended options. Select some you've always wondered about, those suggested by contractors, those you'd love to try someday—put them all on trial. The more possibilities you weigh, the more you'll know about what's right for your house, and the better your chances are of matching your spending limit to the cost of a worthy combination of techniques.

Doing Your Benefit/Cost Analysis

The purpose of the following pages is to show you how to do your own benefit/cost analysis. It's not hard. The vehicle for our evaluation is Evaluation Sheets 1–6. These forms let you gather up all the information you need to derive benefit/cost ratios and net savings for the weatherization schemes you propose. As you can see, there's a sheet for each of your barriers, a sheet for infiltration in case you want to break out air seepage as a separate problem rather than deal with it as part of each barrier's heat loss, and plenty of space to enter data concerning all your weatherization options. (A sample filled-in sheet is shown in Figure 2-3.) This is how you use these forms:

Column 1. Write down each proposed weatherization measure on the appropriate Evaluation Sheet. If applicable, enter the R-value.

Columns 2 and 3. On Evaluation Sheets 1–5, enter your current barrier loss and heating costs. On the infiltration sheet, enter the total wall, window, and door seepage heat loss and heating costs. All the numbers are taken directly from your Work Sheets.

Column 4. Enter an estimate of how long the option will save you money. Usually the life expectancy of a weatherization measure is equal to the life of the house. Check with your supplier or retailer. At any rate, the number you put in column 4 should not exceed the number of years you plan to live in the house.

Column 5. Multiply column 3 by column 4 and enter that number in column 5. If you didn't try any new weatherization measure, this is about how much you'd have to pay in heating costs at present fuel prices for the number of years shown in column 4.

Column 6. Enter your heating cost at present fuel prices for the effective years (column 4) of the option in column 6. You may need to estimate this value for slab floors, basements, etc. But for most barriers, it's a simple calculation. On the appropriate Work Sheet, simply change the annual heat loss formula(s) to reflect the energy saving power of the option. That is, change the transmission formula U-value to allow for added insulation and/or modify the infiltration formula Q-value to allow for a lower seepage rate. Work through the arithmetic to derive a new barrier heat loss total. When you do that, you'll see how much of a difference in Btu's your option can make. Next, multiply that new loss total times your fuel cost per Btu, and multiply your answer times the figure in column 4. Enter that number in column 6. That's how much you'll have to pay for heat lost through the barrier during the time your option is on the job.

1	2	3	4	5	6	7	8	9	10	11
Weatherization Option	Annual Barrier Heat Loss (from Energy Work Sheet)	Annual Barrier Heating Costs (from Energy Work Sheet)	Life Expectancy of Option	Heating Costs of Nonweatherized Barrier (col. 3 × col. 4)	Heating Costs During Life of Option	Potential Savings Derived from Option (col. 5 — col. 6)	Cost of Option	Net Savings (col. 7 — col. 8)	Benefit/Cost Ratio of Option (col. 9 ÷ col. 8)	Priority Order of Cost Effectiveness
Option 1 BLOWN-IN INSULATION R=19	60,726,005 BTU	$485.81	15 YEARS	$7287.15	$2534.65	$4752.50	$700.00	$4052.50	5.8	①
Option 2 PLASTER WALLS R=0.32	60,726,005 BTU	$485.81	15 YEARS	$7287.15	$5205.09	$2082.06	$600.00	$1482.06	2.5	④
Option 3 ASPHALT INSULATED SIDING R=1.46	60,726,005 BTU	$485.81	15 YEARS	$7287.15	$5702.96	$1584.19	$500.00	$1084.19	2.2	⑤
Option 4										

Fig. 2-3. Sample Evaluation Sheet for Exterior Wall. This is what your sheet might look like were you to analyze options for that sidewall in Figure 2-1. The priority numbers in column 11 aren't consecutive because the options have been prioritized along with options for other barriers.

Column 7. Subtract column 6 from column 5 and enter the figure in column 7. This is the potential savings from your proposed weatherization scheme.

Column 8. Enter the cost of your proposed measure, including materials and installation. Only your contractor or supplier knows for sure. With this number and those in columns 4 and 7, you can determine the payback period for your option. Divide the figure in column 7 by the one in column 4 and you'll get the potential annual savings derived from your option. Divide your option cost by that answer and you'll know how many years it will take your proposed scheme to pay for itself.

Column 9. Enter the net savings, which is simply the potential savings gleaned from the option (column 7) minus option costs (column 8).

Column 10. Divide savings (column 9) by cost (column 8) and enter the number in column 10. This is the telltale benefit/cost ratio.

Column 11. Rank *all* your proposed weatherization measures by benefit/cost ratios, from most effective to least. The option with the highest ratio should get a 1, the next highest should have a 2, and so on until each scheme has a priority number. This ranking is an indication of investment quality.

Once you have determined how much you can spend on your energy saving program, you can check off in descending order your top-ranking options until their combined cost matches your spending limit. What you check is what you get: your house's customized weatherization package.

Evaluation Sheet 1: Roof and Attic

1	2	3	4	5	6	7	8	9	10	11
Weatherization Option	Annual Barrier Heat Loss (from Energy Work Sheet)	Annual Barrier Heating Costs (from Energy Work Sheet)	Life Expectancy of Option	Heating Costs of Nonweatherized Barrier (col. 3 × col. 4)	Heating Costs During Life of Option	Potential Savings Derived from Option (col. 5 − col. 6)	Cost of Option	Net Savings (col. 7 − col. 8)	Benefit/ Cost Ratio of Option (col. 9 ÷ col. 8)	Priority Order of Cost Effectiveness
Option 1										
Option 2										
Option 3										
Option 4										

Evaluation Sheet 2: Exterior Walls

1 Weatherization Option	2 Annual Barrier Heat Loss (from Energy Work Sheet)	3 Annual Barrier Heating Costs (from Energy Work Sheet)	4 Life Expectancy of Option	5 Heating Costs of Nonweatherized Barrier (col. 3 × col. 4)	6 Heating Costs During Life of Option	7 Potential Savings Derived from Option (col. 5 — col. 6)	8 Cost of Option	9 Net Savings (col. 7 — col. 8)	10 Benefit/ Cost Ratio of Option (col. 9 ÷ col. 8)	11 Priority Order of Cost Effective- ness
Option 1										
Option 2										
Option 3										
Option 4										

Evaluation Sheet 3: Lower Barrier

1	2	3	4	5	6	7	8	9	10	11
Weatherization Option	Annual Barrier Heat Loss (from Energy Work Sheet)	Annual Barrier Heating Costs (from Energy Work Sheet)	Life Expectancy of Option	Heating Costs of Nonweatherized Barrier (col. 3 × col. 4)	Heating Costs During Life of Option	Potential Savings Derived from Option (col. 5 — col. 6)	Cost of Option	Net Savings (col. 7 — col. 8)	Benefit/Cost Ratio of Option (col. 9 ÷ col. 8)	Priority Order of Cost Effectiveness
Option 1										
Option 2										
Option 3										
Option 4										

Evaluation Sheet 4: Windows

1	2	3	4	5	6	7	8	9	10	11
Weatherization Option	Annual Barrier Heat Loss (from Energy Work Sheet)	Annual Barrier Heating Costs (from Energy Work Sheet)	Life Expectancy of Option	Heating Costs of Nonweatherized Barrier (col. 3 × col. 4)	Heating Costs During Life of Option	Potential Savings Derived from Option (col. 5 — col. 6)	Cost of Option	Net Savings (col. 7 — col. 8)	Benefit/ Cost Ratio of Option (col. 9 ÷ col. 8)	Priority Order of Cost Effective- ness
Option 1										
Option 2										
Option 3										
Option 4										

Evaluation Sheet 5: Doors

1	2	3	4	5	6	7	8	9	10	11
Weatherization Option	Annual Barrier Heat Loss (from Energy Work Sheet)	Annual Barrier Heating Costs (from Energy Work Sheet)	Life Expectancy of Option	Heating Costs of Nonweatherized Barrier (col. 3 × col. 4)	Heating Costs During Life of Option	Potential Savings Derived from Option (col. 5 — col. 6)	Cost of Option	Net Savings (col. 7 — col. 8)	Benefit/ Cost Ratio of Option (col. 9 ÷ col. 8)	Priority Order of Cost Effective- ness
Option 1										
Option 2										
Option 3										
Option 4										

Evaluation Sheet 6: Infiltration

1	2	3	4	5	6	7	8	9	10	11
Weatherization Option	Annual Barrier Heat Loss (from Energy Work Sheet)	Annual Barrier Heating Costs (from Energy Work Sheet)	Life Expectancy of Option	Heating Costs of Nonweatherized Barrier (col. 3 × col. 4)	Heating Costs During Life of Option	Potential Savings Derived from Option (col. 5 — col. 6)	Cost of Option	Net Savings (col. 7 — col. 8)	Benefit/Cost Ratio of Option (col. 9 ÷ col. 8)	Priority Order of Cost Effectiveness
Option 1										
Option 2										
Option 3										
Option 4										

CHAPTER THREE

Insulation: Curbing the Cash Flow

ON a clear winter's day you can see money. Money rising with the vapor coming off uninsulated roofs. Money oozing out of hollow sidewalls that radiate wavy patterns of heat. Heat flow is cash flow. And this chapter is dedicated to the proposition that you can easily curb that flow with your own two hands, or hire out the job without getting swindled. You need to know how to select the right insulation materials, how to judge the feasibility of insulating techniques for your own house, how to actually install the heat-stoppers you need, and how to deal effectively with insulation contractors. You'll learn all that right here.

Whole books have been written on the in's and out's of insulation, so it's easy to get bogged down in advice and data. That's why the information I present is carefully circumscribed. You'll find only the most tested and widely used techniques here, the ones that work best on existing conventional houses (although I'm sure you'll pick up lots of ideas that apply to offbeat installations). The emphasis will be on fighting heat loss, rather than heat gain, because when you do the former, you automatically do the latter. And to coincide with the inspection and calculation procedures of chapters 1 and 2, I'll focus on the insulating of *barriers*, not rooms or spaces.

INSULATION MATERIALS

Table 3-1 is your crash course in insulation materials. It tells you that despite the hundred different packages of insulation you encounter in your building supply store, there are only a handful of different insulating materials, and they come in only three basic forms (blankets and batts are essentially the same type; see Figure 3-1).

All those materials have one thing in common: air. Air, you will recall, makes a fine insulator when it's trapped in small spaces. Therefore all good insulating substances have plenty of air pockets. That's why a 4-foot-thick stone wall has about as much heat-stopping power as a 1-inch-thick blanket of insulation. In order to create these air pockets, insulation is made of fibers, granules, or lightweight "solids." The fibrous materials include fiberglass (glass fibers), rock wool (molten rock fibers), and cellulose (plant fibers). The granular stuff is vermiculite (granules of mica) and perlite (granules of volcanic ash). The "solids" are polystyrene, polyisocyanurate, and urethane, which offer big R-values with a big price tag.

Table 3-1
Approximate R·Values for Insulation Materials

Material	Form	Approx. R-Value per Inch of Thickness	Use	Relative Cost
Vermiculite	Loose fill	2.13	In exterior walls, between ceiling joists, in hollow-core blocks	Medium
Perlite	Loose fill	2.70	In exterior walls, between ceiling joists, in hollow-core blocks	Medium
Fiberglass	Blankets, batts	3.50	Between framing members in walls, floors, ceilings; on crawl space walls	Low
	Loose fill	2.93	Between ceiling joists	Low
	Rigid boards	4.00	On walls, floors, ceilings	High
Rock wool	Blankets, batts	3.50	Between framing members in walls, floors, ceilings; on crawl space walls	Low
	Loose fill	2.93	Between ceiling joists	Low
Polystyrene	Rigid boards	3.57–5.26	On walls, ceilings, floors	High
Cellulose	Loose fill	3.13–3.70	Between ceiling joists, in walls	Low
Urethane	Rigid boards	6.25	On walls, ceilings, floors, rooftops	High
Poly-isocyanurate	Rigid boards	8.00	On walls, ceilings, floors, rooftops	High

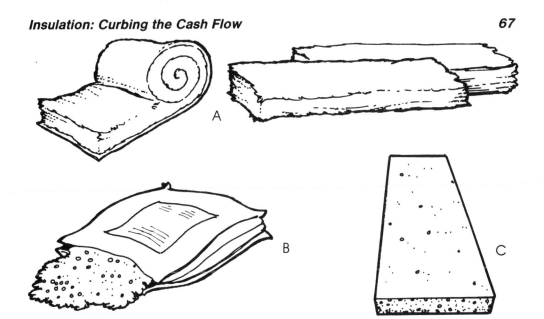

Fig. 3-1. The three forms of modern insulating materials: blankets and batts (A), loose fill (B), and rigid boards (C).

The Vapor Barrier

An invaluable partner to any insulation material is the vapor barrier, an impervious sheeting that resists the passage of moisture. Without it, the value of most installed insulation is worthless. Let's say your sidewalls have no vapor barrier and no insulation. In winter the water vapor that is nearly always present in warm air will flow from your rooms through the wall-board. When it reaches a cool surface (the framing, the wall sheathing), it will condense, turn to water, and damage everything it touches. And if you have *just* insulation in those walls, and no vapor barrier, the damage will be even greater. The vapor will condense in the insulation, destroying its heat-retarding power. It would be much the same for just about any heat barrier you have. *But* if those walls have a vapor barrier on their warm side, the moisture will get stopped before it contacts cold surfaces and condenses.

Blankets and Batts

Blankets and batts are the most popular type of heat-stopper in America (Figure 3-1A). About the only difference between a blanket and a batt is length. Batts are shorter, cut in either 4- or 8-foot runs for easy handling;

Table 3-2
R-Values for Various Thicknesses of Insulation

R-Value	Batts or Blankets		Loose and Blown Fill				
	Glass Fiber	Rock Wool	Glass Fiber	Rock Wool	Cellulose Fiber	Vermiculite	Perlite
			(inches of thickness)				
11	$3\frac{1}{2}$	3	5	4	3	5	4
13	4	$3\frac{1}{2}$	6	$4\frac{1}{2}$	$3\frac{1}{2}$	6	5
19	6	5	$8\frac{1}{2}$	$6\frac{1}{2}$	5	9	7
22	7	6	10	$7\frac{1}{2}$	6	$10\frac{1}{2}$	8
26	8	7	12	9	7	$12\frac{1}{2}$	$9\frac{1}{2}$
30	$9\frac{1}{2}$	8	$13\frac{1}{2}$	10	8	14	11
33	$10\frac{1}{2}$	9	15	11	9	$15\frac{1}{2}$	12
38	12	$10\frac{1}{2}$	17	13	10	18	14

Source: U.S. Department of Agriculture.

blankets are typically 16 to 64 feet long, generally sold in large rolls. Both kinds are made from mineral fibers (fiberglass or rock wool), both come in thicknesses of 1 to 7 inches, both are designed to fit neatly in standard stud or joist spacing (16 or 24 inches), both may have vapor-barrier backings of foil, paper, or plastic. In general, you staple the backed insulation into place because the backing has flanges for that purpose; whereas you wedge the nonbacked stuff between framing members.

As you know, you can't judge insulation by its thickness, but only by its R-value. Fortunately, the R-value of a blanket or batt is usually printed on the package or backing. If you can't find that magic number, don't buy. (For a general idea of the relationship between thickness and R-value for some types of insulation, see Table 3-2.)

When you install any blanket or batt, remember that the insulation itself is noncombustible, but the backing may burn easily. You have to take precautions to see that it doesn't.

Loose Fill

Loose fill (Figure 3-1B) can be either "chopped" mineral fibers (fiberglass, rock wool), granular material (vermiculite, perlite), or cellulose (shredded or ground-up paper). The mineral fibers are easy to install between attic joists, and getting good coverage is a cinch. It's not so simple to get even coverage in walls because the fluffy material snags on nails, wiring, and framing members. You can pour the fibers right from the bag, or hire a contractor to machine-blow them into place. You already know mineral fiber's big selling point: it won't burn.

The granular loose fill isn't used nearly as much as the fibers, probably because vermiculite and perlite (often used in potting soil) are relatively expensive. The R-values aren't much to brag about, either. But when you want to insulate a small, inaccessible space, or fill every nook and cranny of an exterior wall, go granular, if you can afford it.

Cellulose, on the other hand, is cheap and effective, offering more R-value per inch than any other loose fill. Pour it yourself, rent or borrow a pneumatic machine to blow it in, or hire a contractor to do the machine-blowing. Like fibrous loose fill, cellulose is easier to install between attic joists than in walls. (It's tough to evenly fill a cluttered wall cavity with ground-up paper.) But *unlike* the fibers, cellulose can be a fire hazard unless it's chemically treated. Fortunately, the federal government requires such treatment, along with labels on cellulose packages declaring that the contents meet minimum flammability standards. Don't spend your money on *any* brand of cellulose unless you see those labels or some other evidence that the material is safe to install in your house.

Loose fill's biggest drawback is that it has no built-in vapor barrier. Before you pour or blow the material in, you'll probably have to lay sheets of plastic film (polyethylene), asphalt-covered building paper, or foil-backed gypsum wallboard, or apply two coats of moisture-resistant paint.

Rigid Boards

Rigid boards are the superinsulators (Figure 3-1C). You won't find heat-stoppers with heftier R-values than these panels have. Check it out: fiberglass boards, 4.00 per inch; polystyrene boards, as much as 5.26 per inch; urethane boards, 5.30 per inch; polyisocyanurate boards, 8.00 per inch. It's this impressive insulating power that has helped to make them so popular with contractors and homeowners alike.

If you shop for rigid panels, you're bound to run into a baffling array of sizes, from 8-inch squares to 4-$\times$-12-foot sheets, anywhere from $\frac{1}{2}$ to 4 inches thick. Somewhere in the maze, you'll find the size that's best for the job at hand. The job that most homeowners reserve for rigid boards is insulating basement or foundation walls or exposed beam ceilings. Contractors use the panels in even more ways—as exterior sheathing, as backing for siding, as covering for interior wall surfaces, and as underlay for roofs.

The nice thing about the urethane, polystyrene, and polyisocyanurate panels is that they are impervious enough to be their own vapor barrier. The bad part is that they may be combustible *and* give off toxic fumes when ignited. So *always* install these boards so they're separated from your living space by fire-resistant materials. Many building codes require you to cover the panels with ½-inch-thick gypsum wallboard when you apply them to interior surfaces.

Foam

Pump-into-place foam insulation used to be one of the main forms of heat-stoppers. Both major categories of foam—urea formaldehyde (UF) and urethane—offered astounding R-values (about 5 per inch) and built-in vapor barriers. The stuff looked like shaving cream and was injected into place to solidify. The idea was attractive to thousands of homeowners, but foam fell on hard times.

Because the formaldehyde in the UF type was linked to cancer in laboratory rats and because there were flu-like respiratory ailments associated with the fumes from the insulation, the Consumer Product Safety Commission banned the sale of the material in February, 1982. Urethane foam had its own problems. It resisted fire, but once ignited it gave off poisonous gases. And because it expanded greatly after installation and could thus damage framing, it could be used only in limited areas of a house. These deficiencies and the bad press that UF was getting helped push urethane foam toward oblivion. Now you'll be hard pressed to find an installer anywhere who pumps urethane into homes.

HOW MUCH AND WHERE?

When you complete the Evaluation Sheets in chapter 2, you learn what many homeowners would give their eye teeth to know. You garner a legion of facts that pertain exclusively to you and your house, from which you can easily deduce how much insulation to install and where to install it. Customized data like that is always hard to come by. But let's say you've decided to plunge ahead without the analytic approach because you have an aversion to numbers. How then to determine proper insulation levels and placement?

You rely on generalizations, information that applies to *groups* of homeowners, data that pertain only to the "usual" or "average" situation. You encountered some generalizations about levels and placement in chapter 2, such as the FHA-recommended insulation levels, and you'll find Figure 3-2

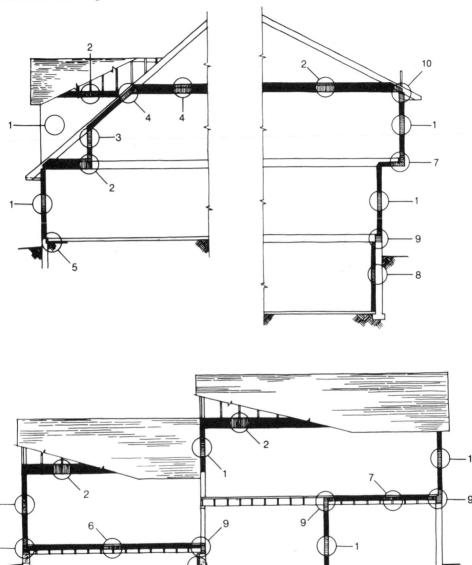

Fig. 3-2. Places that may need insulation: exterior walls (1), ceilings with cold spaces above (2), knee walls when attic space is finished as living space (3), between collar beams and rafters above attic space that's finished as living space (4), around the perimeter of a slab-on-grade (5), floors above vented crawl spaces (6), floors of habitable rooms over an unheated space (7), basement walls (8), on the inside of band or header joists (9), and around pipes and wires where they penetrate to the outdoors (10). (From *Insulation Manual: Homes, Apartments,* 1979, available at $10.00 per copy from the National Research Foundation, Inc., P.O. Box 1627, Rockville, MD 20850)

is a good companion to those guidelines. The big job is to apply the guidelines as best you can to your specific circumstances. You have to find out how much insulation you have now, determine if existing insulation needs to be replaced because it's wet—and read the rest of this chapter. The following pages will help you take into account your house's structural limitations, the feasibility of various installation techniques, and other factors. Just don't expect answers derived from generalizations to have the precision of a computer readout. You'll get good guesstimates, nothing more.

DEALING WITH A CONTRACTOR

Want to hire a contractor to do your insulating for you? Fine. You'll save yourself a lot of time and sweat. But unless you're careful, you could end up shelling out hundreds of dollars for an insulation job that isn't worth a plugged nickel. Or worse. Most insulation contractors do good work, treat their customers well, and turn a fair profit. But far too many installers are dishonest, incompetent, or both. So protect yourself. When you want a true-blue contractor, take the cautious approach.

First, search out several contractors through recommendations from your utility company, homeowners who've had insulation work done, government home improvement programs, or the National Association of Home Builders. You want to hear about companies that have been in business for a good while, companies that are well known.

Next, check out your prospective contractors with the local Better Business Bureau. Ask if anyone has complained about any of them. If there's even one complaint against an installer, cross him off your list.

Then give each bona fide prospect a little quiz. Ask him if his insurance covers your house for damages and his workers for injuries during installation. If he says no, he flunks. Ask him if he will draw up a contract stating the cost of the job, the payment method, the specifications of the bid, and the final appearance of the installation. If he will give you nothing in writing, say good-bye. Ask him if he will conduct an inspection of his work after installation. If he says no, he's off the list.

The contractors who survive this grilling (there should be at least three) are your prime candidates. Ask them for bids and references. Give each prospect the same information about the job (R-value desired, type of insulation, placement, etc.) and make sure he knows that others will bid on the work (nothing like competition to keep down the price). The references should be past customers. Call them and find out what they think of their installation.

When the bids are in and you've checked the references, you can make up your mind. You'll have to live with the insulation job for a long time, so select the contractor who delivers quality workmanship as well as low price.

After you sign the contract with Mr. Right, he goes to work, and so do you. You have to inspect the insulation he installs *and* the way he installs it. Arrange ahead of time to see the stuff he proposes to put into your house. Examine the packaging for R-value, flammability labels, and installation notes. Everything should coincide with the specifications in the contract. If you order loose fill, check the bags for "square footage" data. It tells you how many square feet a bag of loose fill will cover for a given R-value. Knowing that and the square feet to be insulated, you can compute the number of bags needed for the job. And then you can ensure that you're getting your money's worth by either counting the empty bags or keeping track of the bags as the insulation is put in. If there's a discrepancy between the number of bags installed and your computations, see the contractor. And when your installer has finished his handiwork, look it over carefully. Make sure that every square inch has been covered completely, that the insulation is deep enough, that vapor barriers are in good shape and in the right places.

One more thing: Keep a record of your installation, some proof that a certain contractor installed a certain kind of insulation to a certain R-value. Such evidence will come in handy if you ever become dissatisfied with the installation or decide to sell your house.

BUT BEFORE YOU INSULATE

Safety First

Before you begin, take time to consider some safety precautions. According to the Consumer Product Safety Commission, over 2000 houses catch fire each year because faulty wiring ignites thermal insulation. So your first safety drill should be having your house's electrical system checked out by a professional *before* you do any insulating. A thorough wiring inspection will cost you from $25 to $50—but it could save you hundreds of dollars in repairs.

Safety drill number two is making sure your installation (do-it-yourself *or* professional) meets building code requirements. Many state and local codes tell you how far your insulation should be from electrical fixtures and other heat-producing devices. Some codes even specify flammability ratings for insulation. So check it out by calling your local utility, fire department, consumer affairs office, or building code official.

And, please, if you're doing the work yourself, wear the proper clothing and safety gear (discussed further in the following sections), install attic insulation in cool weather or the coolest part of the day (working in a hot attic can cause heat prostration), get your doctor's okay to do the strenuous work an installation demands, and don't smoke while you're installing.

Leaks

Another preliminary worthy of your attention is moisture control. I'm thinking of moisture problems that vapor barriers alone can't solve. If your roof leaks, installing attic insulation is a waste of time. If water seeps into your walls, blowing in cellulose is futile. Moisture reduces the R-value of insulation, causes rot, and weakens framing members. So before you insulate, make sure you've plugged all the leaks.

Ventilation

You must also take steps to ensure adequate house ventilation. In winter a lot of moisture can build up in crawl spaces and attics, and without good ventilation, that dampness can do as much damage as dripping water. You need some natural or forced venting to carry that moisture out of the house. Natural venting implies a simple opening in your house through which air passes; forced venting means a wall- or roof-mounted fan. In general, an unheated crawl space with vapor barrier on the ground should have 1 square foot of natural vent area per 150 square feet of crawl space floor, with a minimum of two foundation wall vents in opposite walls. An attic without a vapor barrier separating it from the rest of the house usually requires 1 square foot of natural vent area per 150 square feet of attic floor; an attic with a separating vapor barrier generally needs 1 square foot of natural vent area per 300 square feet of attic floor.

As you might expect, there are lots of ways to achieve this degree of attic ventilation (Figure 3-3), and lots of variations from the norm. In most houses half the required vent area should be in the soffits and half in the roof or gables. This configuration allows rising air to flow up through the soffits and out the higher vents, carrying moisture to the outdoors. But you can also reduce the area of natural venting by making good use of forced ventilation. You might even ventilate so well that an attic vapor barrier is unnecessary. If you want to be absolutely sure your house is properly ventilated, call a reputable ventilation contractor or your building code officials.

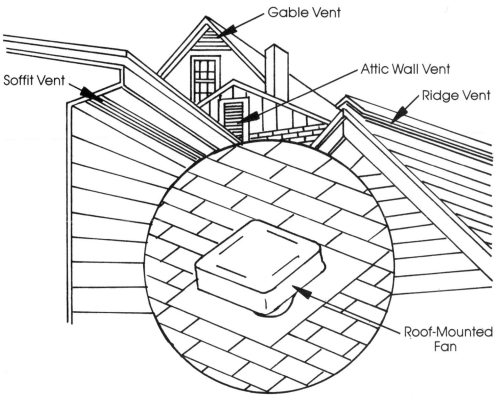

Fig. 3-3. Attic ventilation systems. Clockwise from left: soffit vent, gable vent, simple attic wall vent, ridge vent, and roof-mounted fan. (Source: U.S. Department of Agriculture)

INSULATING ATTIC FLOORS

This section, and the ones that follow, is designed primarily for do-it-yourselfers, and it is based on the premise that the heat barriers you are confronting haven't a speck of insulation. So on the following pages, you'll find a lot of instructions that tell you how to insulate the uninsulated. This is valuable information for *any* homeowner, even the nonhandyman who prefers to let a contractor handle the installation.

So let's begin with an easy job, namely, putting insulation between attic floor joists that don't have flooring. You can use either blankets, batts, or loose fill, and deciding which one will take some thought. It's harder to hand-pour loose fill than lay blankets or batts, easier in close quarters to handle batts than blankets, harder to install a separate vapor barrier for loose fill than use the vapor barrier already attached to batts or blankets, and easier to machine-blow cellulose into place than do any other kind of attic installation. And then there's the R-value to consider. If you want the insulation to ride no higher than the tops of the joists (because you might want to add flooring some day) and still give you a certain R-value, figure carefully. Blankets and batts with their relatively low R-values per inch may give you too much depth; cellulose may fit perfectly.

Blankets or Batts Between the Joists

Let's say you've decided on blankets or batts. To install them safely and efficiently you need to wear the right clothes and use the right gear. Because mineral fibers can irritate your skin, don loose-fitting duds: pants, long-sleeve shirt, and gloves. Because you can easily bang your head into a rafter or a nail sticking through the roof, wear a hardhat. And because the fibers can bother sensitive eyes, noses, and lungs, consider putting on a dust mask or paper respirator and goggles. Don't wear contact lenses—they *never* mix well with insulation fibers.

The necessary gear consists of utility knife (for cutting blankets or batts), trouble light with 50-foot cord (for illuminating attic recesses), tape measure (for checking the length of insulation sections), claw hammer and nails (for insulating the attic access), 2-x-3-foot boards (for laying across joists as temporary flooring), and knee pads (for making all the crawling around a little easier).

You begin installing your blankets or batts in the corner farthest from the attic access hole or stairway. Hang your light there, make sure your tools are close by, and place the 2-x-3-foot boards across some joists. The ceiling between the joists *will not support your weight;* that's why you need the boards. Then lug the insulation packages or rolls up to your corner.

If you're using batts, plan to start laying them between joists at the eaves, working along one side of the attic, then down the opposite side (Figure 3-4). This procedure lets you do any cutting and fitting toward the middle of the attic where you have plenty of elbow room, rather than near the eaves where you can hardly move. If you're installing blankets, you can begin at the eaves and unroll the stuff along the joist spaces as far as you can, cutting and fitting at crossbracings and at opposite eaves. In this way, you can work from one end of the attic to the other.

After you've unwrapped a few packages or rolls, get to it. Position each section so that any attached vapor barrier faces away from you, *toward the*

Fig. 3-4. Slide the batts into the joist spaces, easing them back toward the eaves. (Courtesy Owens-Corning Fiberglas Corporation)

warm-in-winter side of the attic "floor" (Figure 3-5). At the eaves, make sure your blankets or batts completely cover the top plate of the wall below, leaving just enough space for air flow through eave vents (Figure 3-6). Butt sections together tightly, because every gap leaks Btu's (Fig. 3-7). And if possible, leave an air space between the attic "floor" and the bottom surface of the insulation. Air spaces are good for R-values, remember?

To cut the insulation, you'll need one of the 2-x-3-foot boards and your

Fig. 3-5. Positioning the vapor barrier is crucial. Make sure it goes between the "warm" attic "floor" and the insulation. (Courtesy Owens-Corning Fiberglas Corporation)

utility knife. The unfaced (barrierless) batt or blanket is the hardest to handle. Lay it across the board so you'll have a solid surface to cut on, hold the section in place with one hand, and wield the knife with the other. Cut toward you, slicing through the fibers into the wood with short strokes, spreading the gash apart with your free hand (Figure 3-8). If you're not so good at cutting straight lines or if you must slash lengthwise along a batt or

78

blanket, use a piece of scrap lumber for a cutting guide. You slit faced insulation almost the same way you do unfaced, but you make things easier on yourself by cutting it barrier side up.

When you encounter crossbracing or a wood block, cut the insulation and fit it snugly around the obstacle (Figure 3-9). If you try to run the section *over* the block or bracing, you'll create gaps and unevenness in your heat barrier.

And whatever you do, observe the common rules of fire safety. Make sure your insulation doesn't cover anything that produces heat, such as recessed light fixtures or electric fans. I'm sure your building code will have a few words on the subject, but generally you should lay your batts or blankets at least 3 inches away from a heat-producing device (Figure 3-10). If electrical wiring gets in your way, don't disturb it; just try to ease the insulation under it. Although it's usually safe to insulate between framing and chimneys, you should keep vapor barriers at least 3 inches away from them, just as with anything that emits heat.

When you've laid insulation across the entire attic, check the coverage. Look for gaps where sections meet, along the sides of the joists, and at fram-

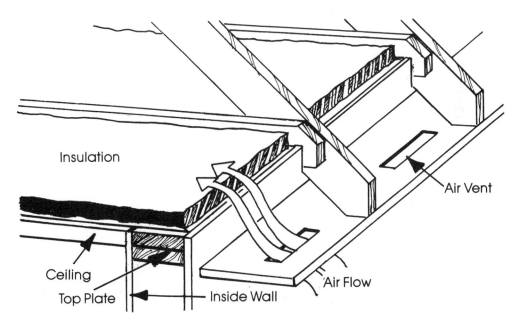

Fig. 3-6. When you set the insulation over the top plates of the house walls, you help to block the flow of heat through those cavities. (Source: U.S. Department of Agriculture)

ing obstructions. After you've certified your handiwork, you can add another layer of blankets or batts if need be, either parallel or perpendicular to the first bunch (Figure 3-11). But remember that your second bed of insulation should *not* have a vapor barrier. It would only *trap* moisture in your blankets or batts. So for that additional layer, either use unfaced insulation or cut lots of holes in the vapor barrier of faced insulation and install facing side down.

Insulating your attic access is saved for last. If you have an attic stairway (pull-down type or any other), it should have a horizontal access door so you can insulate the opening. Nail on blankets or batts (vapor barrier down) or glue on rigid boards. If your attic has a skuttle hole, nail blankets or batts to the lid (Figure 3-12), vapor barrier down, of course.

And *that's* how you insulate a floorless attic with blankets or batts.

Fig. 3-7. Fitting all the blankets or batts together is like trying to work an enormous jigsaw puzzle. Any loose or missing pieces spoil the whole project.

Fig. 3-8. To cut the insulation effectively you have to keep your knife slashing deeper and deeper into the fibrous "weave."

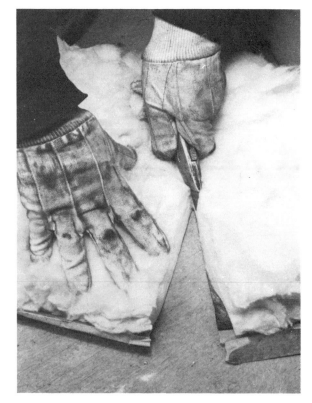

Fig. 3-9. To ensure that the insulation fits tightly around crossbracings or blockings, you'll have to slice it. Usually this means slicing across its width from edge to edge, but sometimes a lengthwise slice is necessary so obstacles can slip into the fibers. (Courtesy Owens-Corning Fiberglas Corporation)

Loose Fill Between the Joists

To do the job with loose fill, you need the same clothes and gear listed earlier plus a few other items. If you decide to pour the fibrous fill, you'll need a cardboard box to fluff it in. And no matter what loose fill you use, you'll want a rake to spread it and some baffles (cardboard or blanket or batt insulation) to keep it in check. If your attic needs a vapor barrier, you'll have

Fig. 3-10. Let your insulation stop at least three
inches away from heat-
emitters like this. Anything
closer is a fire hazard.

to make one with a few rolls of 6-mil polyethylene plastic, some waterproof tape, a staple gun, and plenty of staples.

Start with the vapor barrier. Gather up the makings for your moisture shield, go to a joist space at one of your end walls, and begin fastening the polyethylene between the joists. Flatten out the plastic as you staple its edges onto the joist sides (Figure 3-13). When you have to join two sections of polyethylene, tape the seam. Work your way across the whole attic, watching for gaps as you go.

Next do all the "security" work. Protect your eave vents from clogging with loose fill by installing baffles at the eaves (Figure 3-14). Either staple pieces of cardboard into place or shove 3-foot-long sections of blanket or batt onto the top plates (position the sections as shown in Figure 3-6). Just make sure there's at least 1 inch clearance between your baffles and the roofing. All electrical fixtures and other heat-emitters must be shielded from the loose fill. The best way to do that is to enclose them in a little "house" made of cardboard, blankets, or batts. Staple the "walls" of a cardboard enclosure to the joists (Figure 3-15) and top it off with a temporary cardboard "roof." You can make a blanket or batt house by just scooting sections up to the heat-producer and laying on another for a roof. Just remember to keep the parts of your enclosures at least 3 inches away from the heat sources and *remove the roofs after you insulate.* And because loose fill slips through cracks, be sure to stuff pieces of unfaced blankets or batts between the chimney and the framing, around flues, and in gaps in the attic "floor."

Fig. 3-11. Lay that second layer of insulation right on top of the first—but no second vapor barrier allowed. (Courtesy Owens-Corning Fiberglas Corporation)

Fig. 3-12. A lot of heat can pass through your attic skuttle hole, so be sure it has a heavy layer of insulation attached to its attic side. (Source: Owens-Corning Fiberglas Corporation)

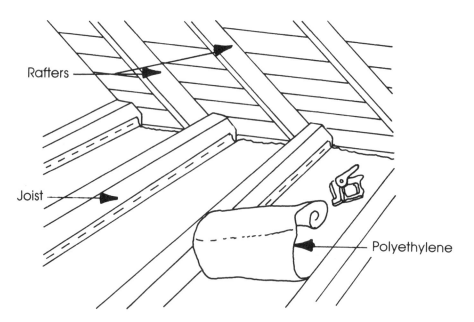

Rafters

Joist

Polyethylene

Fig. 3-13. Try to keep the wrinkles out of the polyethylene as you staple it in place. And be sure to center the plastic in the joist spaces, or else the sheeting will unroll crookedly. (Source: U.S. Department of Housing and Urban Development)

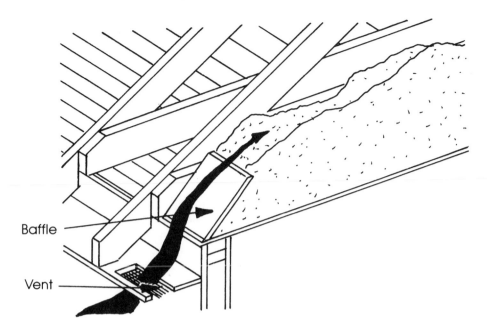

Baffle

Vent

Fig. 3-14. The baffles are vital. They prevent your loose fill from falling down into the soffit and jamming your ventilation. (Source: U.S. Department of Housing and Urban Development)

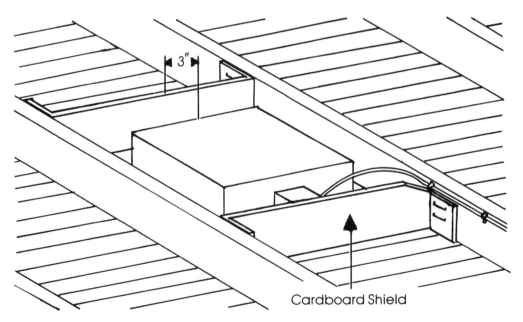

3"

Cardboard Shield

Fig. 3-15. These cardboard separators seem flimsy, but they're strong enough to keep loose fill from spilling against the heat-emitter.

When you've done all that, you can pour or blow your loose fill into place. If you decide to pour, brace yourself for a lot of hard work—a lot of bag toting, a lot of bending over, maybe a lot of fiber fluffing. If you decide to blow in cellulose, you can expect a much easier, faster job, but with a different set of challenges. You'll have to rent or borrow a blowing machine, endure all the dust it kicks up, and recruit a helper.

To pour, begin in the corner farthest from the attic access. If you're using granular insulation or cellulose, just cut the bags open and pour the stuff between the joists, gradually working your way toward the access, checking for correct R-value as you go. The procedure is the same if you're using mineral fibers, except for the extra step of fluffing the insulation before pouring. Fibrous loose fill for pouring (*not* the same material used in blowing machines) will swell to three times its packed volume when you fluff it. And that increased volume is mighty important to the R-value. So before tossing fibers between the joists, throw them in a cardboard box, close the lid, and shake them up. When they've tripled in volume, *then* pour them in the joist spaces. And whether you go granular or fibrous, be sure to rake the insulation smooth and even after it's in place.

To blow in some cellulose, you'll need a crash course in blowing-machine operation, which you should get from the person who supplies the machine. They're too big (about the size of a small washing machine) to set up in the attic, so move them as close as possible to your attic access and hope the hose reaches your joist spaces. The machine gulps down the loose fill, fluffs it, and blasts it through the hose. You just point the mouth of the hose toward your joist spaces, working from an attic corner back to the access. When you get the coverage you want, you start raking.

After all the blowing and pouring is done, insulate your attic access. It's a must—no matter how you weatherize your attic "floor." Just follow the instructions given in the section on blankets and batts.

Attics with Flooring

If you can insulate between joists without flooring, you have all the skills needed to weatherize when there *is* flooring. If you don't plan to use your attic for storage, you can lay unfaced batts or blankets right on top of the floor planks. You need the same clothing and gear used to lay batts or blankets in joist spaces. Simply start at an end wall and lay the sections across the entire floor, butting the pieces snugly as you go (Figure 3-16).

If you don't want exposed insulation on top of your attic floor, you can

Fig. 3-16. In a floored attic, simply shove the pieces into place, fitting them together as tightly as possible. (Courtesy Owens-Corning Fiberglas Corporation)

blow cellulose under the planks, between the joists. All you need is the usual insulation-blowing paraphernalia plus a crowbar. Start by prying up a few planks with your crowbar, the ones on each side of crossbracing or wood blocking (Figure 3-17). This will enable you to blow cellulose throughout the full length of the joist spaces without having to worry about obstructions. Snake the hose into a joist space, stuff the cavity from end to end, and move on to the next one. Since this method doesn't allow for a vapor barrier, you *must* ensure proper ventilation.

87

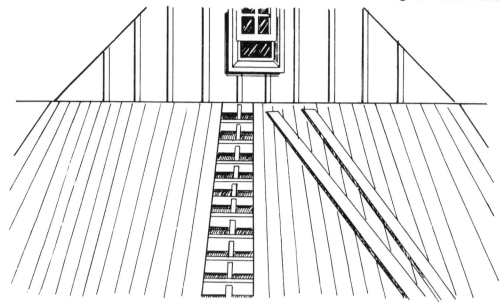

Fig. 3-17. If you pull up the planks that are directly over obstacles beneath the floor, you'll have clear access to all your joist spaces.

INSULATING ATTIC CEILINGS AND WALLS

If you have a finished attic (as defined in chapter 1), this section is yours. It shows you how to insulate your finished attic's knee walls, end walls, covered roof rafters, and collar-beam ceiling. (To insulate behind-the-knee-wall "floors," follow the same procedure described in the previous section on attics with unfloored joists.)

You will need more than one kind of insulation to seal up your finished attic. The knee and end walls require batts; the rafters get loose fill; the collar-beam ceiling takes either one. If your attic must have a vapor barrier, you'll probably want your batts to be faced.

Basic tools and gear are described in the preceding section. But you may have to add equipment to work with wallboard and paneling (ladder, screwdriver, keyhole or saber saw, electric or hand drill, joint tape, joint cement, putty knife, fine sandpaper, coated nails, nailset, wood putty, wood glue), to install faced batts without staples (coat hangers, wire cutters), or to paint on a vapor barrier (oil-base enamel, Glidden's *Insul-Aid*).

The End Walls

The place to begin insulating is at the end walls. Your toughest challenge here is getting at the wall cavities. Some people prefer to cut holes in the wallboard so they can pour loose fill between the studs; others would rather forget the cavities and fasten rigid board insulation right to the wall covering; a few brand the end walls a hopeless case and skip the insulation altogether. You might choose any one of these options. But I must point out their faults. Option one forces you into the difficult task of repairing gaping holes in your wallboard or paneling, and it is obviously not an option for those who need a vapor barrier. Option two usually involves building a frame against the wall to support the rigid panels, gluing or nailing the panels in place, and covering the installed boards with gypsum drywall. That's a lot of work just to achieve an R-value of 8 or 9. Option three, on the other hand, won't work you hard; it will just steal your heating dollars.

Enter option four. With this technique you remove your wall covering, install batts between the studs, and replace the covering. Believe it or not, this approach is probably easier than trying to patch holes in your wallboard or paneling. It is certainly simpler than putting up rigid panels, and cheaper, too. And the method allows for a vapor barrier if you want one, because it is built right into the insulation.

You can pry off your wall covering in less than an hour. Be extra careful in removing paneling to prevent any scratches that will show when you nail it back into place later. With your claw hammer or screwdriver, first pull off all the molding, then pry the panel corners, gently peeling back the sheets, yanking any nails that won't pop out. Don't worry, though, about damaging wallboard. It's unavoidable. Just pull off the baseboard, rip down the sheets with your crowbar, and buy new ones. They're relatively inexpensive and easy to install.

When you remove every scrap of wall covering and make sure the stud faces are free of nails, you can start putting in the batts. To install a faced batt, first cut it to fit snugly against the top plate, then wedge it between the studs (Figure 3-18). Make certain the vapor barrier faces you. Beginning at the top plate, staple the flanges to the sides of the studs, working your way toward the floor, a staple every foot (Figure 3-19). When you come to a fire-block or other crosspiece in the stud space, cut the batt and fit the two sections against the obstruction. Try to slide the batt behind pipes, electrical fixtures, and wiring. If not behind, then around. And remember to keep that flammable vapor barrier at least 3 inches away from heat-emitters. The last thing is to jam the end of the batt against the bottom plate (Figure 3-20). Cut the batt to fit if you have to, to eliminate any gaps.

If you use unfaced (friction-fit) batts, the job is a lot easier. There's no stapling. Just wedge the batts into the cavities against top and bottom plates,

Fig. 3-18. No need to staple the insulation to the top plates. As long as your cuts are accurate, the batts should fit snugly against any top framing, even if it isn't horizontal.

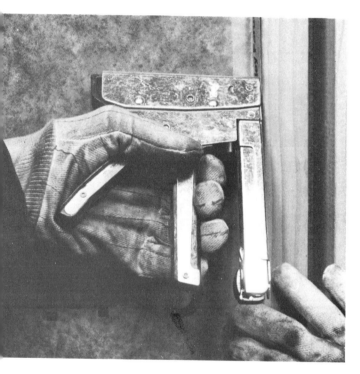

Fig. 3-19. Hold the flanges in position with one hand and do the stapling with the other.

Fig. 3-20. No fastening is required on the bottom plates.

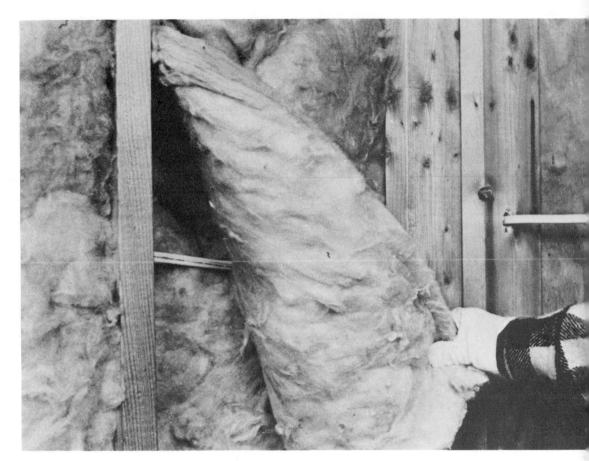

Fig. 3-21. It is best to split friction-fit batts to fit around wiring or fixtures. Forcing it behind the fixture would crush the fibers and diminish the R-value. (Courtesy Owens-Corning Fiberglas Corporation)

and friction holds the insulation where you want it. When you meet a cross-piece, cut and fit just as with faced batts. But when you encounter something like wiring or junction boxes, split the batts with your knife and lay the insulation on both sides of the obstructions (Figure 3-21).

No matter what kind of batt you install, be sure not to miss the narrow spaces and crevices around door and window framings and the skinny stud spaces at the corners of the room. Cut up batts to fit into the larger places, and pack scraps of batt into the little ones (Figure 3-22). If your attic needs a vapor barrier, staple polyethylene over those smaller insulated spaces and put faced batts into the larger. Facing will take staples just as well as flanges.

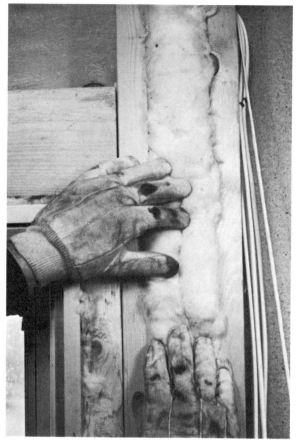

Fig. 3-22. Crushing the fibers is unavoidable here. The main thing is to fill up the holes with as much insulation as possible.

When you have weatherized all you can, cover up with paneling or wallboard. Replacing your paneling is a matter of nailing the sheets back into their old positions, countersinking the nails with your nailset, filling the holes with wood putty, and retacking the molding. Installing new wallboard is a little more involved. Stand the sheets into position and nail their edges to the studs, driving the nailheads just below the panel surfaces, a nail every 7 inches. When you have to custom-cut a sheet, slice the face paper with your knife, place the cut along the edge of a board, sliced surface facing up, and bend the panel downward. The wallboard should snap apart along your cut. When you finish all the nailing, use a putty knife to squeeze joint compound along the seams where the panels meet, evening up the compound with the surrounding surface (Figure 3-23). Then take the knife and press joint tape into the seam compound, smoothing as you go. Let the compound dry, apply a second coat, wait for it to dry, put on a third, and wait some more. Level out the third coat with fine sandpaper and the job's done. The paint or wallpaper is up to you.

And that's the story on insulating your end walls. If you look at Figure 3-24, you'll see why weatherizing the other parts of your finished-attic barrier is a little more complicated. The knee walls, outer attic joists, ceiling and rafters are all interconnected—and usually tough to get at. But there are ways.

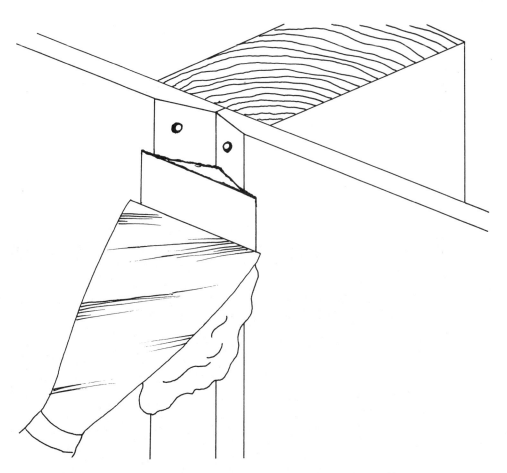

Fig. 3-23. When finishing wallboard seams, it helps to use a putty knife with a wide blade that can easily straddle the surfaces on either side of the seam.

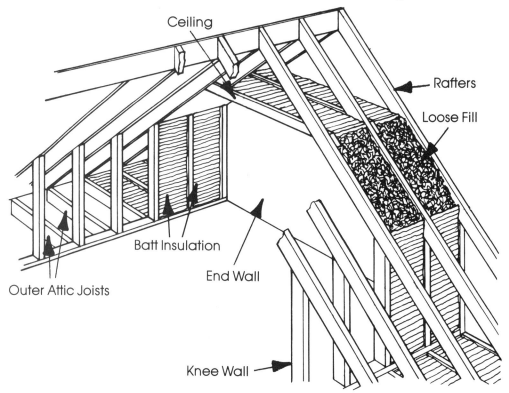

Fig. 3-24. Cutaway view of a finished attic. (From *How to Cut Heating and Cooling Costs,* by Peter Jones, © 1979 by Butterick Publishing. Reprinted by permission of New Century Publishers, Inc., Piscataway, New Jersey)

The Knee Walls

Concentrate first on getting through the knee walls. Chances are, you'll have to cut an access door in each of them. Start the cut by drilling a $\frac{3}{8}$-inch hole at the top of the knee wall, near the sloping rafter ceiling. (Stay clear of electrical wall fixtures, though.) Then take your saber or keyhole saw and cut from the hole horizontally to the nearest stud, then downward alongside it to the baseboard or bottom plate (Figure 3-25). Make another horizontal pass, then up and over again to the hole. The rectangle you cut should fall right out.

Once you get behind those walls, start weatherizing. Insulate the outer-attic joist spaces the way you would any other joist spaces. If your attic doesn't require a vapor barrier, wedge friction-fit batts between the knee wall studs as though you were sealing up an end wall. Make sure that the insulation fills the stud spaces from bottom plate to roof sheathing. If you do need a vapor barrier, squeeze faced batts into the cavities (from plate to roof) with the facing toward your finished area, then secure the insulation with wire braces (Figure 3-26). (Cut your own batt-holders, $15\frac{1}{2}$ inches long, from coat hangers.) Arch the braces from stud to stud, bowing them against the batts. Tension does the rest.

The Rafters

You insulate the knee walls before taking on the rafters because you need a backstop for the rafters' loose fill (see Figure 3-24). The method you use to get to the rafters depends on how that collar-beam ceiling is put together. How *is* your ceiling put together? If the collar beams are about 4

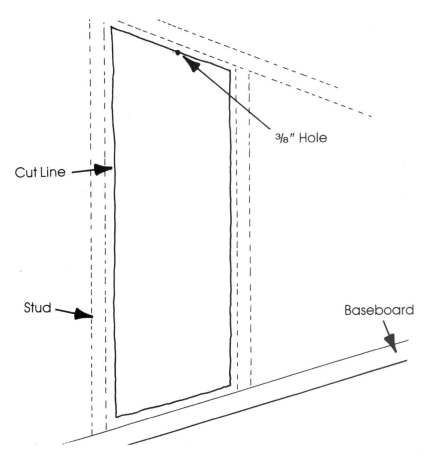

Fig. 3-25. Cutting an access through the knee wall.

feet long or longer, there's probably enough room above them to crawl around and pour or blow loose fill down the rafter cavities. Using what you already know about cutting through knee walls, you can carve a trap door in the ceiling for access. (Never mind the vapor barrier; tend to that *after* you weatherize your rafters.) But if the beams are short, you'll have to cut access holes at the upper end of the rafter cavities, just below the collar beams (Figure 3-27). Because patching a lot of little holes is so time consuming, you'll probably want to slice off an entire swath of drywall on each side of the beams, and then pour or blow in the insulation right up to the holes.

Putting loose fill between your rafters is just like installing it between your attic floor joists. You blow in cellulose; you pour in anything you want (though the granular may cover better). Be sure to check behind the insulation in your knee walls to make sure the loose fill isn't getting past your backstop.

And the vapor barrier? It's nearly impossible to install one in your rafters—there's not enough room, not enough light, and too many nails sticking through the roof. So you forget about *installing* and start thinking about *painting.* Buy some Glidden's *Insul-Aid* paint or a quality oil-base enamel and

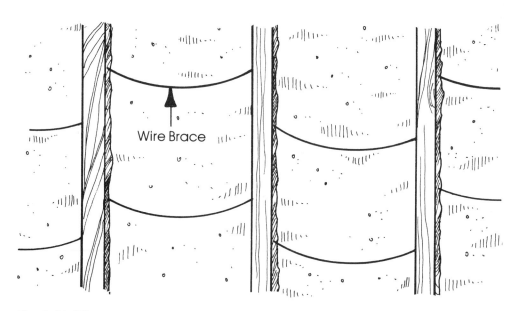

Wire Brace

Fig. 3-26. When you press batts into your knee walls with the vapor barriers facing the living space, you place the flanges out of your reach. So you have to do the fastening with the coat hanger braces.

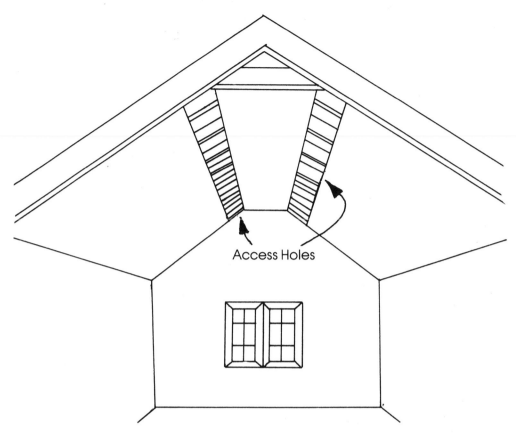

Access Holes

Fig. 3-27. These holes may not look very pretty, but they provide you with your only practical access to the rafter cavities when the collar beams are short. Replacing the wallboard cutouts is much like replacing wallboard on your end walls.

apply it to the drywall of your rafters and ceiling. If you need extra moisture protection, you can paint a vapor barrier on the knee and end walls, too.

The Attic Ceiling

If you're lucky enough to have ample working room above the collar beams, insulating between your attic ceiling joists will be fairly straightforward. Using the techniques you learned from the previous section, you can blow in cellulose, lay batts, or pour in the loose fill of your choice. The only snag is the vapor barrier. If you need one, you can't pour or blow in loose fill until you've crawled up there through your access hole and stapled polyethylene between the joists. And you can't lay a batt unless it's faced.

Insulating an attic ceiling with *no* elbow room above it is *not* so straightforward. One look at Figure 3-27 tells you that. Your best bet might be to boost some short vapor-barrier-faced batts up through those top access holes and cram the insulation between the joists. Or you could close up the holes (see the previous discussion of wallboard installation), cut a hatchway in the ceiling board, snake a blowing-machine hose up there, and blast cellulose from one end of the roof peak to the other. You would then have to get your vapor barrier out of a paint bucket.

Finishing Up

The last chore is insulating and closing the access doors. The hatchway up top is the easiest one to take care of, so begin there. Glue a couple of 1-x-2's to the back of the hatchway's cutout (Figure 3-28). The boards should extend over the edge of the drywall about 2 inches. After the glue has dried, cover the cutout back with blanket or batt insulation, with the vapor barrier against the drywall. Glue the insulation to both cutout and boards. Let dry, slide the whole thing up through the hatchway, and fit it into the opening, finished side down. You can then let it be or seal up the cracks as you would any other wallboard joints.

Now to close that knee wall opening. First you have to build a backstop to give the wallboard cutout something to rest against when you fit it back

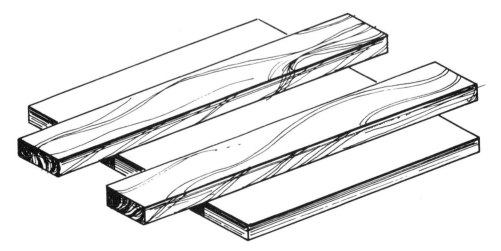

Fig. 3-28. A homemade hatchway lid.

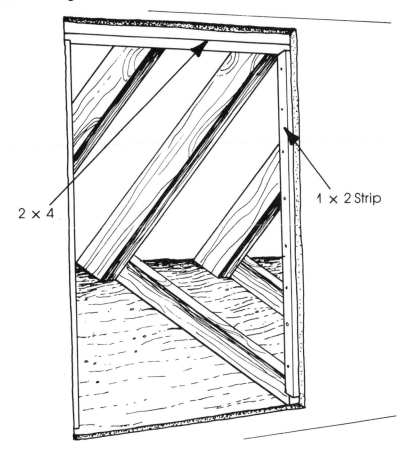

Fig. 3-29. A simple backstop for a knee wall cutout.

into the wall. At the top of the access hole, nail a 2-x-4 between the studs (Figure 3–29). Let the 2-x-4 rest against the drywall, about $\frac{1}{2}$ inch below the drywall's cut edge. Then nail a 1-x-2 along each passageway stud, making sure the 1-x-2's are even with your 2-x-4. That's your backstop. Glue some batt or blanket insulation to the back of the cutout (vapor barrier facing the wallboard) and let dry. Set the cutout into the wall opening, nail it to the backstop, and treat the seams with joint cement and tape (see the previous discussion of wallboard installation).

INSULATING SIDEWALLS

The time to insulate your sidewalls is before the house is finished being built. The contractor is almost done; the framing is up, the roof is on, the exterior coverings are in place, and the studs are ready for drywall. *This* is the time to insulate your sidewalls. Catch them *before* they're covered with wallboard and you can insulate them the same way you would attic end walls. If you must weatherize them *after* the wallboard is on, the job gets twice as hard and much more expensive.

The same goes for installing a vapor barrier, which is one thing that every sidewall must have. Before the walls are covered, you can staple faced batts between the studs, which results in instant moisture guard. After the walls are covered, you have to improvise. You'll have to either paint a moisture shield over the wallboard or cover it with 6-mil polyethylene sheeting, stapling the sheeting right to the drywall, nailing panels of $\frac{3}{8}$-inch wallboard over that, and painting or papering to finish.

So what are the options for the homeowner who must insulate a houseful of closed-up walls? You could rip down your wallboard and lay in batts or blankets. But you would be, in effect, gutting your house. That means a heap of hard work, dust, cash outlay, and general inconvenience. Unless you're planning a house-wide remodeling campaign, this approach is probably more trouble than it's worth.

If your house has "balloon" framing, you might be able to insulate your sidewalls with granular loose fill. A true balloon wall has open cavities that run from the foundation to the attic. There are no top plates or crosspieces to block the stud spaces. So you can go up to the attic and pour perlite or vermiculite down those cavities, filling them from bottom plate to brim.

But your balloon walls may have obstructions in them. To find out for sure, you'll have to slip into some protective clothing, put on some knee pads, tie a long string around a golf-ball-sized weight, and get up to the attic to check the stud spaces. Drop the weight down the cavities and see if it snags on something before it reaches the bottom plate. If it does, you know that the insulating job is a lost cause. If all is clear, and you can stand the bending over, you can haul the bags of granular up there and pour. Backbreaking work. If you choose this route, cut open one bag at a time. After all, granular costs too much to spill.

Another option is to hire a professional to blow cellulose or mineral fiber insulation into your wall cavities. The project may be a bother, it may be expensive, it may be against the do-it-yourselfer's creed. But it may be the only option some homeowners have. If you've read the section on insulation materials, you already know the pros and cons of the stuff that gets blasted into your walls. You should also know something about how the

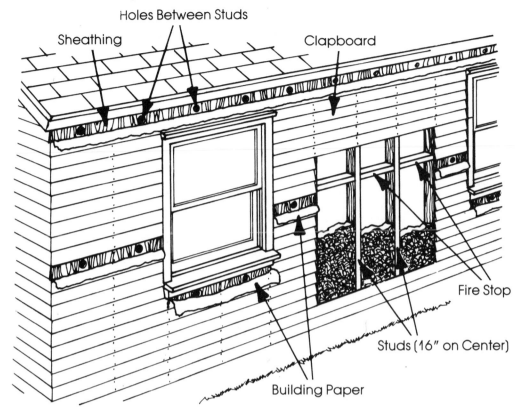

Fig. 3-30. Installing cellulose or mineral fiber insulation in your sidewalls means cutting lots of openings to accept the machine's hose. (From *How to Cut Heating and Cooling Costs,* by Peter Jones, © 1979 by Butterick Publishing. Reprinted by permission of New Century Publishers, Inc., Piscataway, New Jersey)

installation is done. Drilling all those holes, of course, is the first big step (Figure 3-30). The contractor makes the openings in either the outdoor or indoor surfaces, depending on your preferences or the composition of the walls. If you can't stand the thought of holes in your wallpaper, if the exterior covering is easily patched, or if you have shingles that are simple to remove and replace, the contractor will probably drill outdoors. The outer covering is supposed to be peeled back or temporarily removed before the drilling begins. But sometimes the contractor skips this step, and the result is unsightly walls full of poorly-disguised plugged holes. Make sure you know how the work will be done before signing the contract. If you're planning on refurbishing your inside wall surfaces, or your outside surfaces are masonry, you'll probably want those holes drilled indoors. At any rate, because the installer must create openings between each pair of studs and above and below each crosspiece, there will be *lots* of hole-plugging and wall-patching after installation.

It's not unheard of for a homeowner to try to save some money by taking on the professional's job by drilling those holes or blowing in loose fill or both. But unless you're highly skilled, that approach could be a big mistake. Before drilling, you'd have to plumb for fireblocks, heating pipes, and electrical wires. Miss something and you could be in lots of trouble. To drill indoors, you'd have to move or offset all electrical boxes. And getting the right insulation density is no easy trick, either.

If none of these insulating methods appeals to you, you can have insulated siding or insulation boards applied to your sidewall exterior. But because these coverings can be expensive and have relatively low R-values, they may not be cost-effective for you. If their R-values plus the R-values of your sidewall materials don't surpass recommended levels (Figure 2-2), beware. To be on the safe side, consult your utility company and your state or local government-sponsored weatherization program—or submit the insulation to the benefit/cost analysis of chapter 2.

INSULATING CRAWL SPACE WALLS

In general you'll want to take on the project of insulating crawl space walls if you plan to use your crawl space for storage, if you need to give your below-floor water pipes extra protection against freezing, or if your region's design temperature is 10°F or less. You can insulate only your crawl space walls, or you can double the defense against the cold by weatherizing the house floor, too (see next section). (If the above criteria don't apply or your crawl space needs all the ventilation it can get, you should consider insulating *just* the floor.)

But whatever tack you decide on, don't forget my earlier advice about checking with your local building code officials and other experts. That tip is especially important here. In some sections of the country the insulation may need a vapor barrier; in others it may not. The following techniques are well suited to most regions, but not to all (like Alaska, Minnesota, and northern Maine). A phone call could save you a lot of grief.

To do the job right you'll need your standard protective gear (including goggles and hardhat), trouble light, claw hammer, long nails, utility knife, tape measure, duct tape, handsaw, $\frac{1}{2}$-x-$1\frac{1}{2}$-inch wood nailing strips, 6-mil polyethylene sheeting, bricks or stones, and fibrous blankets.

The polyethylene is meant for the ground in your crawl space, and it's mandatory if you want to keep moisture out of the insulation you install. Dampness seeps out of the dirt and into the space, unless you stop it with the plastic. So lay that sheeting before you do anything else. Use the trouble light to illuminate your work, but keep light, wires, and insulation off wet ground. Unroll the polyethylene across the dirt, laying it from wall to wall, cutting it with your knife at the end of each run. Overlap each section about 6 inches and tape the ends up onto the walls (Figure 3-31). To hold the plastic in position, lay the bricks or stones here and there along the seams. Wear soft-soled shoes and tread lightly to avoid putting holes in your vapor barrier.

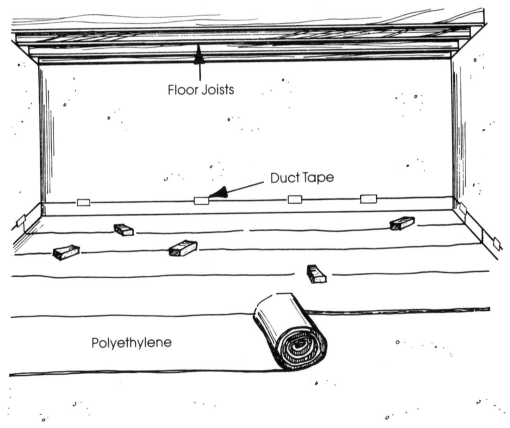

Fig. 3-31. A polyethylene vapor barrier for a crawl space's dirt floor.

Start insulating at the header joists, the framing beams that rest on your foundation walls and run perpendicular to your floor joists. Measure and cut small pieces of blanket to fit tightly against the headers, then shove the insulation into position, vapor barrier toward the crawl space (Figure 3-32). After that, saw the $\frac{1}{2}$-x-$1\frac{1}{2}$-inch nailing strips into pieces about twice as long as your joist spaces. Cut blankets so they'll hang from the subfloor to the ground and 2 feet across the floor. Place the blankets on the walls over the the header insulation (vapor barrier if required, facing you,) and fasten them to the sills with the wood strips and nails (Figure 3-33). Drive the nails deep enough to grip the sill, but not far enough to crush the insulation. Butt the blankets against one another and anchor the trailing 2 feet with the bricks or rocks.

Now work on the two walls that are *parallel* to your floor joists. You won't need any little pieces of blanket here because there aren't any floor joists to get in your way. Cut your blankets so they can cascade from the band joists (the foundation beams that run *with* the floor joists) to the ground and along the floor 2 feet (Figure 3-34). With your wood strips, nail the top of the blankets directly to the band joists. And when the blankets overlap

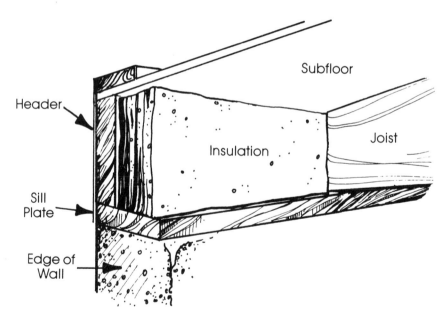

Fig. 3-32. If you cut the insulation properly, it should wedge firmly against the headers without staples or nails. (Source: U.S. Department of Housing and Urban Development)

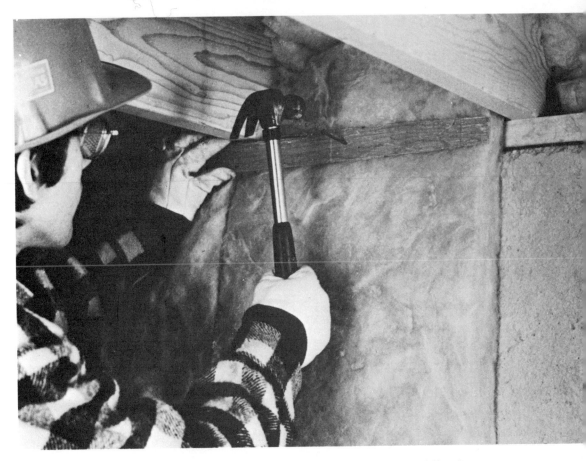

Fig. 3-33. Be sure to hang the blankets straight so they'll fit together tightly when you nail them up. (Courtesy Owens-Corning Fiberglas Corporation)

at the corners of the crawl space, slice off the excess. Spread a few rocks or bricks about and you're finished.

INSULATING FLOORS OVER UNHEATED SPACE

Floors over unheated spaces are the ones your feet tell you about every winter—the ones over the unheated garage, workshop, porch, or crawl space. These floors can siphon off thousands and thousands of Btu's from your house every year. And you can probably insulate any one of them in less than 5 hours.

The job requires the usual garb; coat hangers or staple gun, staples, and thin wire; trouble light; wire cutters; tape measure; 6-mil polyethylene

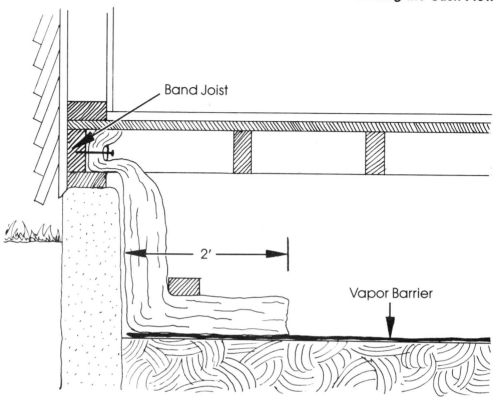

Fig. 3-34. Be sure that the insulation presses hard against the subfloor, and be careful not to squash the blankets by nailing too deep. (Source: U.S. Department of Housing and Urban Development)

sheeting (if you insulate the floor above a crawl space); ladder (if the floor is out of reach); utility knife; duct tape; and faced batts.

If you're going to weatherize your crawl space "ceiling," lay the polyethylene on the ground first. If you don't, moisture will ruin the insulation for sure. See the preceding section for instructions.

Insulating your floor is just a matter of fastening batts up between the joists. Do one joist space and you know how to do them all. Start by setting up your trouble light and other trappings near a header joist. Wedge a batt into one of the joist spaces, vapor barrier side up (Figure 3-35). Fold up the end of the batt and slide it right against the header (Figure 3-36). If you can, leave an air gap between the batt facing and the subflooring above (because you know what a good insulator confined air is). Then fasten the batt into position. You can brace the batt up with 15½-inch wire braces cut from coat hangers (as in figure 3-26) or staple thin wire to the bottoms of the joists in a crisscross pattern. Either way, just make sure the insulation doesn't sag and leave gaps.

Do the same for all the adjacent joist spaces until you have batts all along that header. Then butt other batts against those, fastening and fitting, working your way to the opposite header, where you fold up the batt and push it against the header. If you run into plumbing pipes or the like, measure and cut the batts to fit snugly around the obstacles. Be sure none of the batt facing is exposed to heat-emitters or is clogging combustion air openings for your furnace.

Once you've insulated from header to header, you can start thinking

Fig. 3-35. Usually the batts are fat enough to stay put for awhile once you push them into place. (Courtesy Owens-Corning Fiberglas Corporation)

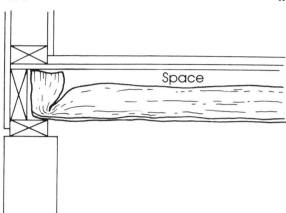

Fig. 3-36. This end-fold helps slow down the heat that passes from the living spaces through the floor and header. (Source: U.S. Department of Agriculture)

about stuffing scraps of batt in crevices, or nailing a plywood or wallboard covering to the joist bottoms, or taping pieces of batt around ducts and pipes. That first trick is standard operating procedure; the second is optional; the third is a must—uninsulated heat ducts and pipes in a cold space waste your Btu's.

Postscript: You can insulate flat or mansard roofs the same way you insulate floors. After all, these atypical roofs have joists, too.

INSULATING BASEMENT WALLS

The techniques discussed here apply to *bare* masonry walls, the kind most basement owners have. These methods, however, do *not* pertain to homeowners living in far northern or southern climates. Extreme frost penetration in places like Alaska or Minnesota can cause your foundation to heave if you insulate according to these instructions. And in areas like Texas and Florida where cooling bills can be bigger than heating bills, the last thing you want to do is insulate basement walls. In hot climates, the ground can actually help cool down the house by drawing off heat from the structure. Insulation would just short-circuit that process. When in doubt, get some answers from local professionals.

Before you even think about insulating, clear up any moisture problems. If your basement walls are wet, it will do you no good to weatherize, because the dampness will undo your work. (For a detailed discussion of how to get rid of basement dampness, see *Weatherproofing*, pages 21–23 and 26–39, published by Time-Life Books.)

After fixing any leak problems, there are two ways to proceed. If your basement walls are smooth, flat, and plumb, you can glue rigid boards directly to the masonry. It is actually a fairly easy job, although there is plenty of cutting and fitting involved. But if your walls are too rough to take adhesive, you'll have to build a frame against the masonry and staple batts between the frame members. Erecting that wooden skeleton is the biggest chore; the insulating itself is a cinch.

Regardless of the method you select, you'll need your protective clothes, utility knife, masonry nails, small sledge hammer, tape measure, handsaw, claw hammer, and framing nails. For the rigid-board procedure, you should also have duct tape, wood nailing strips (2 inches wide and as thick as the rigid panels), caulking gun, wood battens or metal brackets, screwdriver and screws, paneling adhesive (specially formulated to work with your insulation), and panels.

The Frame-and-Batt Method

For the frame-and-batt approach, add these to your equipment list: 2-x-3 studs, coping saw, plumb bob, level, coated nails, staple gun, staples, and faced batts.

Figure 3-37 shows you how your wall frame should look. To build framing like that on your own masonry, start with the top and bottom plates (beams). With your masonry nails and sledge hammer, nail 2-x-3's to the floor at the base of the walls. Use the level to insure that the plates are perfectly horizontal. Near the ceiling, with framing nails and claw, nail 2-x-3's to the bottom of the overhead floor joists. (On the walls that are parallel to the floor joists, you'll have to install the uprights first and then nail the top plates to them.) To install all these 2-x-3's you'll need to do some cutting and measuring at the corners of the room and plenty of checking with the plumb bob to make sure the top and bottom plates are parallel.

The positioning of the upright studs is critical. They must fit snugly between the plates *and* be spaced to properly accommodate the batts. Depending on the width of your batts, you'll need to maintain a stud-to-stud distance of either 16 or 24 inches.

On walls that run at right angles to your floor joists, you can nail the studs to the plates. Where the walls run parallel the floor joists, you'll have to nail the studs to the masonry and crown them with top plates later. Keep the framing true by using your plumb bob and level. And if you have to install the studs around pipes or other obstructions, get out the coping saw and custom-cut the framing to fit (Figure 3-37).

Fig. 3-37. A 2-x-3 frame for masonry wall insulation. (Courtesy Owens-Corning Fiber-glas Corporation)

Once your frame is up, you can insulate. The place to start is at the header and band joists. Peel the facing off some batts (for fire safety), slice them to fit between the floor joists, and press the sections against the headers (Figure 3-38). Then strip a few more batts and staple them along the band joists, slicing where needed to ensure a close fit between subfloor and top plates.

The rest of the job is much like insulating an attic end wall. Simply staple batts between the studs (vapor barrier toward you), and install wallboard or paneling over the framing. (You have to install these coverings because the facing is flammable. Any molding or other finishing touches are optional.) The one notable difference between this insulating technique and others like it is the length of the batts. In most climates, you need only lay batts from the top plates to 2 feet below ground level. Only in very cold regions do you insulate from plate to plate.

Fig. 3-38. You want these small pieces to touch all the adjacent surfaces—the joists, headers, and subfloor. (Courtesy Owens-Corning Fiberglas Corporation)

The Rigid Board Method

If you're installing rigid insulation boards, the first thing you do is grab a hammer and nail the wood strips at the top and bottom of the walls. This mini-frame will give you something to nail the wallboard to after you put up the rigid panels. So you'll want to make sure that the strips will be about flush with the installed panels. Use masonry nails to fasten the bottom strips to the base of the walls; use framing nails to secure the top strips to the foundation sill plates.

Then make sure that *all* the panels are going to fit properly on the walls *before* you start squirting adhesive. Your walls may not be the same height everywhere. Measure and cut the panels to fit around windows and pipes. Score the boards with your utility knife, apply a little pressure, and they'll snap along the score line.

Next take up the caulking gun, spread beads of adhesive across a section of the wall in wavy patterns, and press a panel into position. Don't be stingy with the glue; you want plenty of holding power. Repeat with all the panels. Then cover all the joints with duct tape. And don't worry about a vapor barrier: The boards themselves are fine moisture stoppers.

Wait a few days to let the adhesive get a good grip. Then you should install $\frac{1}{2}$-inch-thick gypsum wallboard over the panels. The gypsum retards the spread of flames, and it's an absolute must. Nail it right to the wood strips with your coated nails. (See the section on attic ceilings and walls for installation instructions.) And to ensure that the wallboard stays put in a fire after the adhesive has melted away, you'll need to anchor the gypsum along its top edge; the strips alone won't do the trick. You can install metal brackets or wood battens to hold the wallboard to the sill or floor joists. Use screws here for solid fastening.

INSULATING SLAB FLOORS

Slab floors lose so much heat along their edges that a little perimeter insulation can make an enormous difference, a difference you can detect with your feet on a winter's morn. And that's good news because perimeter insulation is the only hope for most homeowners who want to stop the flow of Btu's through their slabs. You obviously can't insulate *under* the slab, and usually can't *on* the slab, so you weatherize the edge.

You'll need to wear some work clothes and buy or beg the following: shovel, wire brush, rigid panels, paneling adhesive (made to work with

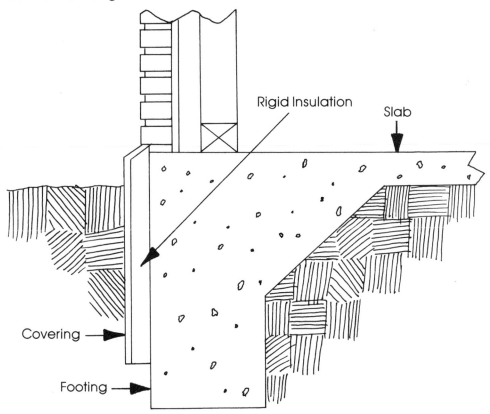

Fig. 3-39. Rigid insulation on a slab-on-grade. (Courtesy Dow Chemical U.S.A.)

your insulation panels), caulking gun, utility knife, covering material (exterior plywood, asbestos-cement board, building paper, stucco, etc.), and the tools to apply it (sledge hammer, paintbrush, etc.).

Your mission is to attach the panels to the outside surface of the slab, where it descends to the footing, running the panels from the bottom of the siding or masonry to the frostline (Figure 3-39). To do that, of course, you'll have to dig, and dig, and dig—probably no more than 2 feet down, but all around your house. Once you've bared the wall, you'll need to brush it off so the adhesive can do its work.

After the brushing, spread beads of adhesive on the wall and press the panels into place. Make sure the top edges of the panels are as close as possible to the siding or masonry. Measure and cut where necessary.

Then protect the panels with a covering of plywood, building paper, stucco, whatever your building code allows. Below ground, the panels need a good defense against moisture; above ground, they need a shield against sunlight. Some coverings can be attached with the same glue you use on the insulation, others with masonry nails, and a few (like stucco) are mopped on. Consult your siding dealer or builder for specifics.

The final step is the easiest—replacing the soil from the trenches. Pack it tight against the panels.

CHAPTER FOUR

Weatherstripping and Caulking: Plugging the Leaks

WHO in his right mind would leave a house window wide open all winter long? A few lovers of fresh air might, but most warm-blooded creatures would cringe at the thought. Yet every year thousands of homeowners commit the equivalent sin: they leave the crevices in their house wide open. It's true: the leaks in the average home waste as much heat as an open window. That isn't so surprising when you think of crevices in terms of area. A $\frac{1}{16}$-inch-wide crack around a door frame equals a $3\frac{1}{2}$-inch-square hole. A $\frac{1}{8}$-inch-wide door-frame crack equals an 8-inch-square opening.

Bless weatherstripping and caulking. There's no way to have an energy-efficient dwelling without them. Wherever two different surfaces meet (house siding and window frame, for example), crevices will inevitably appear. The differing surfaces expand and contract at different rates, and all the movement sooner or later widens the seams. Caulking must come to the rescue. And wherever doors and windows swing or slide, there's bound to be gaps in their seals when closed. Weatherstripping has to fill the space.

When you shop for caulking and weatherstripping, don't let the price tags make up your mind for you. These two energy-savers are not only good investments—they're all relatively cheap. You could probably strip and caulk your whole house for less than $40. The thing that should sway you is product information. You need to know how effective the stuff is, how long it will last, how to install it. This chapter is a good guide to that kind of data. I discuss the most useful, most popular types of weatherstripping and caulking, include notes on their durability, and give you general guidelines on installation. Armed with this information, you should be able to walk into a home center or hardware store with a good idea of what you want and why, and you will be able to read the labels with a discriminating eye.

WINDOW WEATHERSTRIPPING

You probably know precisely which windows need weatherstripping. The cold blast through the crevices leaves no doubt in your mind. But if you're the least bit uncertain, take a hint from chapter 1, and use a lit candle to check for leaks. Ease the flame along the window cracks, wherever there's a joint between movable and stationary parts. A flicker says weatherstrip.

Mind you, you might have to tear off some old weatherstripping to make way for the new. You might even want to make some window repairs. After all, it's a monumental waste of time to weatherize a window that begs to be refitted to its frame or needs its panes puttied airtight.

When you set out to shop for weatherstripping, take your window measurements along with you so you'll know how much to buy. In the language of chapter 1, "window measurements" means "crack length"—the length of the chinks around the window perimeter, around any movable section, and along any meeting rails.

Tension Strips

No doubt you've seen these energy-savers in the sash channels of countless windows (Figure 4-1). They are what their name suggests: metal or plastic strips that do their job through spring tension. When fastened in place, they automatically stretch against an opposing surface, sealing out air. Some of them are flat; others have a cross section shaped like a V; still others are shaped like a lazy S. They're all the same as long as the tension is there. And while it is there, the strips do an excellent job of retarding infiltration. You can use them on nearly every kind of window—double-hung, sliding, casement, awning. And the nice thing is, the strips have low visibility. Once you install them, you'll hardly notice them.

Give the metal strips an A for durability. They'll outlast just about every other weatherstripping on the market. Give the plastic strips a B+. They'll never be as tough as metal, but they're a close second.

In general, tension strips are a little harder to install than most other

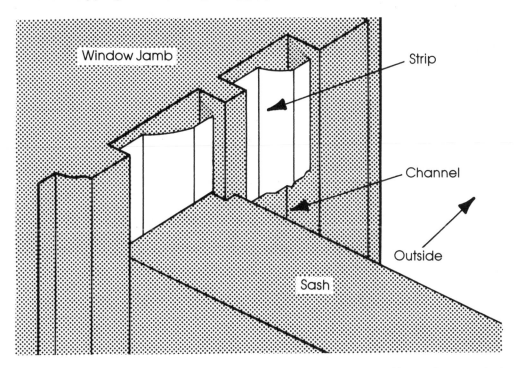

Fig. 4-1. Tension strips fasten to the sash channels and squeeze themselves against the edge of the sashes.

kinds of weatherstripping. On double-hung windows you usually start by cleaning the surfaces that will receive the strips, namely, the sash channels, the bottom of the lower sash, the top of the upper sash, and the inner side of the upper sash's bottom rail (Figure 4-2). You want to clear away every bit of loose paint, dirt, and grease.

Install the vertical strips first. The usual procedure is to measure and cut four strips, two for the inner sash channel, two for the outer. (You'll need tin snips to sever the metal strips; scissors to cut the plastic ones.) Measure from the base of the inner channel to 2 inches above the topside of the bottom rail of the upper sash, then cut all four strips to that measurement (Figure 4-3). After that you can slide each strip into place to check the positioning before fastening. Raise the lower sash and slip the weatherstripping into the inner channels, making sure that the flared flanges face *away* from you (Figure 4-4). Then lower both sashes and do the same fitting in the outer channels. You may have to custom-cut the strips around window hardware, like hinges and sash pulleys.

Fig. 4-2. A thorough cleaning is the pre-requisite for a good installation.

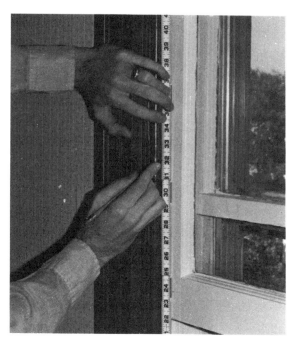

Fig. 4-3. The extra 2 inches of weather-stripping should stick out beyond the sashes when your window is closed.

Fig. 4-4. Position the strip's nail holes or adhesive backing *toward* you.

Fig. 4-5. Be sure to drive tacks flush with the channel surface.

How you attach the strips into place depends on the strips themselves. Some are tacked down; some have adhesive backing so you can press them onto surfaces (Figure 4-5). And regardless of how you fasten them, you always have to bend out their flared ends to increase the spring tension and maximize the seal (Figure 4-6).

Attaching the horizontal pieces is a lot less bothersome. First measure the bottom rail of the lower sash, from channel to channel. Then cut three strips to that measurement. Tack or press one cross strip to the bottom side of the lower sash, with the nailing flange toward you, and repeat the procedure on the topside of the upper sash (Figure 4-7). Fix the third strip to the inside of the bottom rail of the upper sash, nailing flange up, flared edge down (Figure 4-8). The last step is to bend out the strips to boost the tension.

If you can handle all that, you can install tension strips on the other window types, too. After all, the sliding window is nothing more than a double-hung turned on its side. Simply weatherstrip the parts that move. Casement and awning windows have basically the same configuration with the same opening action, and they require the same simple weatherstripping approach. Attach tension strips around the perimeter wherever you can (Figure 4-9). Just be sure to position any nailing flanges or adhesive backing toward the side where the window swings open.

Adhesive-Backed Foam or Rubber

No doubt you've seen this form of weatherstripping, too. It comes in "belts" backed by pressure-sensitive glue for easy installation (Figure 4-10). You buy it in rolls of precut widths, thicknesses, and lengths. If you install it right, it'll give you an effective low-visibility seal against drafts and dust.

Keep in mind that there are several types of foam weatherstripping, and they are not all of the same strength. There's vinyl foam (the toughest of the lot), neoprene sponge (the runner-up), sponge rubber (with medium strength), and foam polyurethane (the weakest of all). You can't expect much more than a 2-year effective lifespan from any of them. Plus there's the problem of sticking power—over time, foam materials may peel away from surfaces. The worst offender seems to be sponge rubber.

The rubber (nonfoam) strips are usually as durable as the vinyl foam strips, and they generally do a fair job of resisting sunlight discoloration, water absorption, and freezing. But they often share the fault of sponge rubber foams: they can come unstuck.

There's one handicap that all these self-adhesives share: poor abrasion

Fig. 4-6. This procedure is vital: no tension, no closure against the weather.

Fig. 4-7. The trickiest part here is aligning the strip with the edge of the sash.

Fig. 4-8. The tacks must be flush or they'll snag the top rail of the lower sash.

Fig. 4-9. Facing the strip's flared edge in the right direction is critical; position the nailing flanges toward the open side, and the flared edge toward the closed side.

resistance. Installed where they're likely to rub against a sash or frame, they'll wear away in a hurry. On double-hung windows, that means you should install them only on the bottom of the lower sash and the top of the upper sash. On sliding windows, install them only where the sash strikes the vertical channels. On awnings and casements, install them around the whole window perimeter but only where the window unit is supposed to contact the frame.

Self-adhesive strips are a hot sales item, partly because they're so easy to install. Make sure that the receiving surface is clean and dry, cut the strips to the correct length, peel back the protective backing, and press them into position (Figure 4-11). That's all there is to it. You'll find that they do a pretty good job of sealing nonuniform cracks.

Fig. 4-10. There are so many different kinds of adhesive-backed stripping on the market, you're sure to find some that suit you.

Fig. 4-11. Installing a foam strip on the bottom of a lower sash is the easiest weatherstripping job of all.

Tubular Gaskets

If you glued a length of garden hose along the bottom of one of your lower sashes, and then closed the window, the hose would compress and block out the gales. You'd have an awkward but effective weatherseal. In fact, you'd have a tubular gasket, one that resembled many of those down at your hardware store (Figure 4-12). The store-bought versions, though, are highly specialized and diverse. Some are made of rubber; some of plastic. Some are hollow; some have cores of sponge rubber or polyurethane. Some have lips or flanges for nailing; some have adhesive backing.

But they have common denominators, too. They all work well on most window types, and they all get fair marks for durability. They're also unsightly when installed because they're always in full view. That's why most people attach them to their window *exteriors*. And it's why some home-owners are tempted to paint the strips, a costly mistake for sure. Paint stiffens them and robs their sealing power.

As with most kinds of weatherstripping, the best place to find specific installation instructions for these gaskets is on the package. There's a huge array of tubulars out there, each with its own peculiarities. In general, though, attaching the stuff to double-hung windows is usually a straight-forward job. Most often it involves tacking the strips to the outdoor side of the window along the edges of the upper and lower sash channels (Figure 4-13), along the top rail of the upper sash and bottom rail of the lower (Figure 4-14), and along the bottom rail of the upper sash (Figure 4-15). You can generally treat sliding windows in the same fashion. Casement and awning windows usually take the gaskets all around the edge of the pivoting frames (Figure 4-16).

Standard Felt Strips

Felt strips are one of the oldest and cheapest breeds of weatherstripping you can buy (Figure 4-17). They are nothing more than thick bands of wool, cotton, or other fabric that you fasten along air-seeping crevices. The strips can be as narrow as $\frac{3}{16}$ inch, as wide as $1\frac{1}{2}$ inches, and as long as 25 feet. Some are installed with tacks, some with an appropriate store-bought glue, some with their own self-adhesive backing.

But they have their limitations. For one, they are not very durable. They

Fig. 4-12. Tubular gaskets are compressible, yet tough.

Fig. 4-13. You can tack to the sash or the frame, as long as the seal is good.

Fig. 4-14. Appearances don't count here; it's the fit that matters.

stand up to abrasion or Mother Nature better than self-adhesive foam does, but worse than just about anything else. That goes for wool felt, too, which usually outlasts felt made from other fibers. Felt strips are not very compressible, either. In fact, they compress so little that you can use them only on gaps that are uniform. So you can apply them to just about any window— but only where friction is minimal, where wet weather can't penetrate, and where cracks are even and straight. On double-hung windows, that means only on the bottom of the lower sash and the top of the upper sash; on sliders, only where the sashes meet the side channels; on casements and awnings, only around the perimeter of the pivoting frame.

Installing felt with an adhesive backing is just like installing foam or rubber strips. Clean, cut, peel, and press. Attaching felt with a store-bought glue is virtually the same job—just make sure to get a glue that bonds with felt and your window surfaces. And tacking on the felt is very much like nailing the tubular strips. You measure and cut the felt, tack down one of its ends, and nail it every 3 inches, keeping the strip taut as you go (Figure

124

Fig. 4-15. A lot of infiltration gets in past the bottom rail of the upper sash, but a tubular gasket ought to stop most of it.

Fig. 4-16. When you close a pivoting window, the tubular should press tightly against the window trim.

Fig. 4-17. The stripping that your grandparents used: standard felt. (Courtesy Stanley Tool Works)

125

Fig. 4-18. Drive the tacks in as far
as they'll go.

4-18). Because the felt will stretch a bit, you may have to slice off some excess
at the end of the run.

Reinforced Felt or Vinyl Strips

If you were to clinch standard felt or a tubular gasket in a flexible aluminum clasp, you'd have a reinforced strip (Figure 4-19). The reinforcement
gives the felt or vinyl a little more toughness, and it ups the price. Other
than that, there isn't much difference between regular felt or vinyl and their
reinforced cousins.

Reinforced vinyl, like standard tubulars, has high visibility when
installed, is usually nailed into place, and generally goes on window exteriors. You can tack it on the same window types, on the same cracks, and in
the same manner as you would any tubular. You just have to pack some tin
snips to cut it to size.

Reinforced felt, like standard felt, comes in rolls, is fastened with nails
or glue, must be installed in protected spots, and can go on most kinds of
windows. But it installs the way the tubulars do. On double-hung windows,
you attach it to the top of the upper sash, the bottom of the lower sash, and
the bottom of the upper sash (Figures 4-20 and 4-21). Certainly this kind of

Fig. 4-19. Reinforced felt and vinyl: added stiffness for traditional weather-stripping materials.

Fig. 4-20. When you tack reinforced strips to the top of the upper sash and bottom of the lower sash, you have to work with the window closed to ensure proper fit.

Fig. 4-21. When you install reinforced felt on the bottom of the upper sash, make sure that the felt protrudes just enough to press against the top rail of the lower sash.

Fig. 4-22. On casement and awning windows, the felt must rest firmly against the pivoting frame when the window is shut.

interior installation will be an eyesore, but exposing the strips to the elements will destroy their effectiveness in no time. On casement and awning windows, you affix the strips along the exposed edge of the window perimeter (Figure 4-22). Use tin snips to cut it to size.

Hinged-Window Strips

Hinged windows, such as casements, awnings, and others, have their own specialized sorts of weatherstrips. They may or may not be better for hinged windows than tension strips, tubulars, or any other general type, but they hold out the promise of an exceptional seal. They are worth looking into if your hinged windows whistle with the breeze. You'll find at least two types. One type, available from Thermwell, Inc., is nothing more than a vinyl gasket with a U-shaped groove that slips onto the lip of the window frame (Figure 4-23). You slice the gasket to the proper length and slide it onto the frame lip. If you do the job right, you'll get a near-airtight seal when you close the window against the vinyl. The other type, available

Fig. 4-23. This grooved gasket can seal even those casements that need a facelift. As long as the paint on the frame lip is sound, the gasket will stay put.

Fig. 4-24. Stanley's answer to the leaky hinged window is a skinny, self-adhesive gasket.

from Stanley Hardware, is a rubber-plastic miniaturized version of the tubular gasket (Figure 4-24). It fits around the window edge or frame lip just as a foam strip might. You clean the receiving surface, peel off the backing of the self-adhesive, and press the strip into place. Both kinds of hinged-window weatherseals have good durability ratings—nearly as good as metal tension strips.

DOOR WEATHERSTRIPPING

The first step in sealing leaks around doors is a seepage check. Which doors are letting in the frigid air and spewing out the Btu's? Your eyeballs and a lit candle tell all. Just don't overlook the not-so-obvious offenders, like that door to the unheated basement, the one to the unheated garage, the one to the unheated room.

When you've spotted the culprits, take a closer look. Do they fit right, or do they bind when you open or close them? Might as well forget about weatherstripping until the fit problems are cleared up. You may have to plane or sand the door edges or adjust the hinges, but repair you must. I don't mean that your doors have to be perfectly square inside their frames, just that they work freely. A door that opens well but doesn't meet the doorstop quite right can be sealed with the proper weatherstripping.

You'll also need to check out existing stripping on your leaky doors. Can you adjust it for a better seal? Some door weatherstripping can be tinkered with; some can't.

While you're investigating, you might as well measure door crack length, door thickness, and door-bottom-to-floor height, unless you've already recorded this data on your Work Sheets. You'll need those numbers when you shop for the leak-stoppers. Door weatherstripping, which can be either top-and-side strips or "door bottoms," usually comes in standard sizes, and selection is a lot easier when you know your door measurements.

The Old Reliables

Most of the window weatherstripping discussed on the preceding pages is perfectly suited for doors, too. Tension strips, adhesive-backed foam or rubber, tubular gaskets, standard felt, reinforced felt or vinyl strips—these are as effective on jambs and stops as they are on window frames or sashes. Installed correctly, they'll last as long on doors as they will on windows. Getting them on is easy, because you install them on your frames' top and sides where you have plenty of working room.

Nail, glue, or cut the strips as you would window seals. Tack or glue

Fig. 4-25. The flared edge goes next to the doorstop; the nailing flange goes toward the indoors.

tension strips right to the jambs (top and sides) along the doorstop (Figure 4-25). For the latch side of the doorway, cut the stripping to fit around the strike plate. After installation, pry up those flared ends a bit to increase the spring tension. With the adhesive-backed foam or rubber and the standard felt, seal along the doorstop on the latch side and top (Figure 4-26) and down the jamb on the hinge side (Figure 4-27). You fasten reinforced strips to the doorstop, too, but on the frame's top and *both* sides (Figure 4-28). And as you might expect, you attach most tubulars exactly the same way you do the reinforced strips. You can, however, secure a few of them to the face of the stop instead of the side (Figure 4-29).

Rigid Strips

These top-and-side weatherseals are generally just vinyl or foam gaskets backed by wood or stiff aluminum (Figure 4-30). If you look hard enough, though, you may be able to find a few consisting of a single piece of vinyl. But whatever they're made of, rigid strips always go on your door's top and side stops and usually give you a decent seal against the winds—better than felt and as good as the tubulars.

One disadvantage is that rigid strips are probably the most expensive

Fig. 4-26. When your door closes, it compresses the stripping and chokes off the air flow.

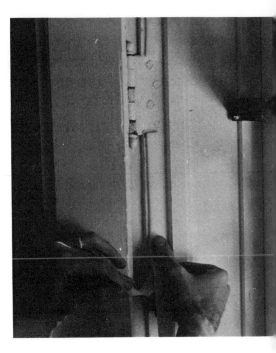

Fig. 4-27. You want to be sure to weatherstrip along the entire length of the jamb, except where the hinges might crush the stripping.

Fig. 4-28. Position the strips so the felt or vinyl presses lightly against the door when closed.

Fig. 4-29. This installation is simple, but you must be certain that the door will close properly when the stripping is in place.

top-and-side leak-sealers you can buy. It's that extra measure of rigidity that hikes the price. Another disadvantage is that most rigid strips are *less* durable than reinforced gaskets, *less* durable than tension strips. A case in point is certain types of wood rigid strips, those with the plastic glued directly to the edge of the wood. Too often the gasket peels away from the backing when the weather gets mean. However, the strips that secure the gasket in a groove in the wood don't have that problem.

Fortunately, rigid strips come in kits. One kit for one door. Usually you'll get two long strips for the side stops, a shorter strip for the upper stop, and maybe some screws or nails for fastening. With the wood-backed strips you could get either nails or screws; with the other rigid strips you'll probably get just screws.

Installing rigid strips is a lot like attaching reinforced gaskets. You cut the strips to size with a saw (handsaw for the wood, hacksaw for the aluminum), fit them against the doorstop and the closed door, then screw or nail them into place (Figure 4-31). After installation these seals are visible,

Fig. 4-30. Rigid strips are highly compressible weatherstripping with backbone.

Fig. 4-31. Positioning is crucial: when you close the door, its edges must push gently against the strips.

but you can paint them to blend in with the rest of your door. That is, you can paint the *wood or aluminum backing;* to paint the gasket is to destroy it.

Door Sweeps

Door sweeps are the most popular of the so-called door bottoms, those hard-working weatherseals designed to fill the gap between the underside of your door and the floor. The typical sweep is a plastic or fiber gasket gripped by a wood, vinyl, or metal strip (Figure 4-32). You attach it along the bottom edge of your door and the gasket presses against the threshold (Figure 4-33). Sweeps are inexpensive, fairly durable, and highly effective. About the only thing wrong with them is their visibility. You usually have to install them on the inside of your door, and it's hard to miss them there.

When you shop for sweeps, you'll want to keep an eye out for two things: (1) package instructions that tell you on which side of a door the sweep belongs, and (2) slotted screw holes in the holding strip. The first bit of information is important if you're concerned about visibility; the second

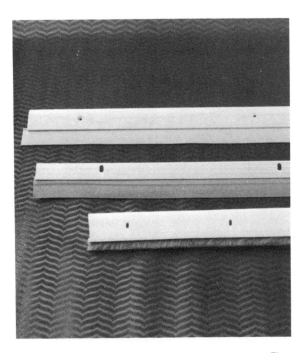

Fig. 4-32. Common door sweeps. The effectiveness and durability of the gasket is of prime importance.

Fig. 4-33. Adjust the gasket to exert light pressure on the threshold.

item is significant if you want to be able to adjust the sweep to compensate for wear.

Installation usually requires measuring the distance between the door-stops, sawing the sweep to fit that measurement, fitting the strip against the door so it lightly touches the threshold, and fastening it in place with screws. You can do the same thing with doors that don't have thresholds, too. You just have to be sure that the sweep doesn't drag across the carpet.

Door Shoes

Door shoes are a variation on the sweep theme. Their most common form is a plastic or aluminum channel fitted with a vinyl or fibrous gasket (Figure 4-34). The channel slides onto the bottom edge of your door, and the gasket presses against the threshold when the door is shut. As long as the threshold presents an even surface for the gasket, you should get an almost airtight seal. To guarantee such wind-blocking compression, you can even buy thresholds designed to complement the workings of a door shoe.

Fig. 4-34. Standard door shoes act as draft-stopping extensions of your door.

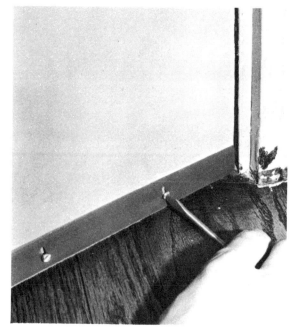

Fig. 4-35. The critical chore is getting the right pressure between threshold and gasket.

Door shoes are about as effective, durable, and visible as the sweeps. You can buy shoes in standard sizes to fit most exterior doors, usually 36 inches long and $1\frac{3}{4}$ inches wide.

Before you make for the nearest supplier of door shoes, better check the clearance between the bottom of your door and the threshold. If it's between $\frac{3}{16}$ and $\frac{1}{2}$ inch, you won't have any problem installing most types. If it's less than $\frac{3}{16}$ inch, you may have to saw or plane the door bottom to make room for the shoe. If it's more than $\frac{1}{2}$ inch, a door shoe alone may not be able to fill the space effectively.

If you don't have to cut away at your door, installing a shoe will be an easy 15-minute job. Saw the shoe to fit between the doorstops, slip it onto the door bottom, fit the gasket gently against the threshold, and screw the shoe into position (Figure 4-35). The channel's screw holes will probably be slotted so you can adjust the shoe up or down after you've set the screws.

Automatic Door Bottoms

Automatic door bottoms are sweeps with a brain. They know to lower their gaskets against the floor or threshold when you close the door and to raise them automatically to clear the carpet when you open the door. It's all done by spring action. Figure 4-36 shows you one of the simplest of the species. It consists of a flexible vinyl sweep, a pivoting aluminum holding strip, a rigid plastic mounting piece, and a small metal spring. When the

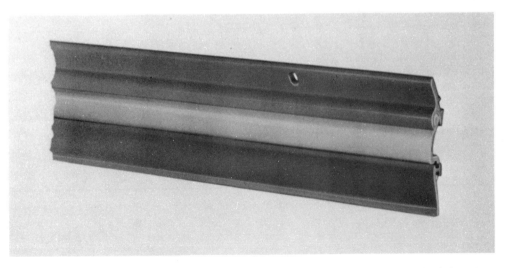

Fig. 4-36. Stanley's aluminum-vinyl automatic. (Courtesy Stanley Tool Works)

whole thing is fastened to the bottom edge of your door, that little spring will ensure that the holding strip and sweep pivot upward (Figure 4-37)—unless there's something to push them down. That something is a nylon roller attached to the doorstop on the latch side of the door (Figure 4-38). Open the door: the sweep springs clear of your carpet. Close the door: the nylon roller forces the sweep to compress against the threshold.

There are more complex automatic door bottoms. Some are mortised into the bottom of the door; some have metal casings that house the retractable gasket. But they all do basically the same job: they save your carpet and themselves from wear. Whether simple or complicated, almost any automatic door bottom will match a regular sweep in effectiveness and visibility, but they probably can't outlast standard sweeps. The moving parts make them more vulnerable to breakdown.

Most of these weatherseals are installed on the exterior side of the door, in plain sight. Generally, you saw the stripping to fit properly between the doorstops, screw it to the bottom of the door so the gasket lightly touches the threshold or floor when the door's closed, and then attach the roller or

Fig. 4-37. The sweep needs to kick up just enough to miss the carpet.

Fig. 4-38. Align the roller with the holding strip to provide proper pivoting action.

other fixture that helps activate the sweep-raising. You want to be careful that the sweep doesn't push too hard on the threshold or floor. Too much pressure wears out the spring in a hurry.

Vinyl-Gasket Thresholds

As energy-savers, vinyl-gasket thresholds are far superior to wooden thresholds and a world better than no threshold at all. They're essentially metal moldings with vinyl insert strips spanning their top face (Figure 4-39). When your door properly closes over one of these thresholds, the door bottom compresses the vinyl and makes an airtight seal. You can use the gaskets in conjunction with sweeps, door shoes, and automatic door bottoms. The only durability problem you'll encounter is the wear and tear of foot traffic on the vinyl. You can counter that worry, however, by replacing the insert when it starts to lose its sealing power.

Your most important installation consideration here is door-bottom-to-floor clearance. These thresholds come in various heights to accommodate different under-door gaps, and if you can match a threshold height to your door's clearance, you've got it made. If your door has too much clearance,

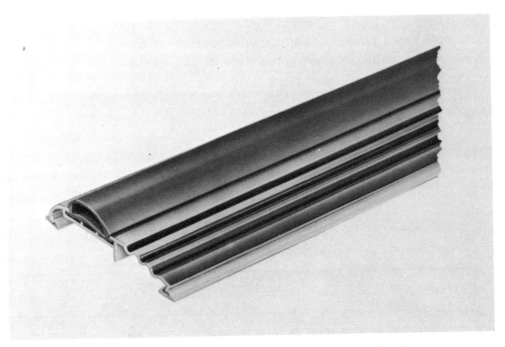

Fig. 4-39. Stanley's aluminum-vinyl threshold. (Courtesy Stanely Tool Works)

you'll have to do without this kind of weatherseal. If it has too little, you'll have to slice a piece off the bottom of your door. If you plan on combining one of these thresholds with a sweep or similar door bottom, you may need even more clearance.

So the first step in installing a vinyl-gasket is to remove the door from its hinges and take care of whatever door-trimming is necessary. If you need to take off $\frac{1}{4}$ inch or less, use sandpaper or a plane. If more than $\frac{1}{4}$ inch, use a handsaw or power circular saw. And while you're at it, you might want to bevel the door bottom about $\frac{1}{8}$ inch for a more dependable seal (Figure 4-40). This procedure is worth trying even if you don't need to trim your door for clearance.

Next, you need to remove any existing threshold. If you own a wooden one, you'll have to pry it up. If its ends are wedged under the doorstop, you can saw through them, lift up the center section, and chisel those end pieces from beneath the stop (Figures 4-41 and 4-42). If you have a metal threshold, simply unscrew it and ease it out.

To fit your new threshold into position, you'll probably have to cut it to length with a hacksaw. You may even have to saw the doorstop so the ends of the threshold will slip beneath it (Figure 4-43). If you have no existing threshold, you can either saw the doorstop to fit around the vinyl-gasket or clip the vinyl-gasket to fit around the doorstop (Figure 4-44).

After the cutting is done, you can set the screws, slip in the vinyl insert, and test your work by opening and closing the door (Figure 4-45). The insert should rest gently against the door bottom when the door is closed, and drag slightly when the door is opened.

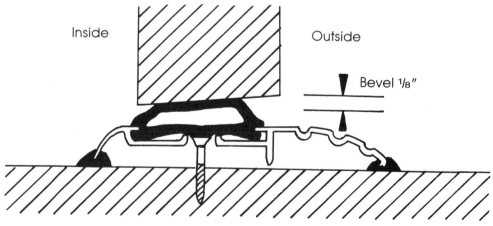

Fig. 4-40. A $\frac{1}{8}$-inch bevel isn't much, but it's enough to create a tighter fit between gasket and door bottom.

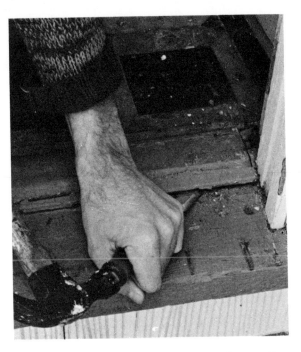

Fig. 4-41. Popping out the center section usually requires a chisel, but a crowbar will do.

Fig. 4-42. A couple taps from your chisel will probably be enough to dislodge these end sections.

Fig. 4-43. For a good fit, you won't need to saw off more than ½ inch.

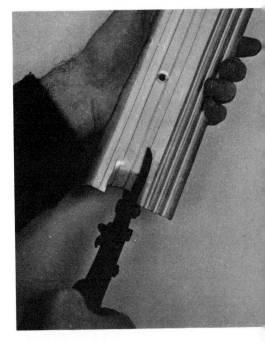

Fig. 4-44. To trim the weatherstripping, tin snips are the tool of choice.

Fig. 4-45. The vinyl-gasket at work.

CAULKING

You may recall from chapter 2 that caulking was not included in the roster of "big" weatherization strategies. But you mustn't conclude from that deliberate omission that caulking is a "little" energy-saver. The procedure usually can't beat out the biggies in slashing fuel bills, but it does a respectable job. Believe me, a 10% reduction in household heating expenses is respectable. That's what caulking can do for you. And it's always cost-effective. Buy any caulk you care to have, plug the cracks that suck the heat from your house, and the sealing job will pay for itself in a year.

Where to Caulk

Here is a checklist of targets, places where you're most likely to find crevices that need caulking. The places in this list are, in part, a recap of the ones you encountered in chapter 1.

Where exterior door frames and sidewalls meet.
Around exterior water faucets and electrical apparatus.
Where utility lines, vent pipes, and flues penetrate the ceiling below
    an unheated attic.
Between sidewalls and foundation or crawl space walls.

Where dissimilar sidewall coverings meet.

Where window frames meet sidewalls.

Around sidewall vents, exhaust fans, and utility entrance lines.

Where chimneys or masonry meet sidewalls.

At corners formed by siding.

Where sidewalls and roof connect.

Around basement windows.

Between porches and sidewalls.

Two cautions: don't seal both the inside and outside of your sidewalls if you live in extremely cold and humid climates, and don't plug up drain holes. The northern Maine seacoast and areas of Canada have the kind of climate I'm referring to. In those areas you have to make sure that any moisture that gets in the sidewall cavities can escape to the outdoors. If you seal up both the interior and exterior wall surfaces, dampness could get trapped inside and eventually cause mildew or rot. So you caulk the inner surface and plug up only the large openings of the outer skin. In other regions, you can caulk inside and outside as you please. And as for those drain holes, I mean the little openings in some kinds of sidewalls (those covered with brick veneer or siding, for instance) and storm windows. Those apertures allow condensation to seep away. Plug them up and you're asking for moisture troubles.

Caulking Materials

When you go hunting for caulk at your local hardware store or home center, you may run up against as many as forty different brands. It's a crowded market, and sorting through the avalanche of possibilities can be as tough as the caulking job itself. It helps, though, to know what characteristics you're looking for in caulking. Consider these:

1. Durability. How long will that caulking job last? Will that caulk stay flexible and give you a good seal over the long haul, through all kinds of weather? These are the most significant questions you can ask about a caulking compound. After all, if you caulk your house with stuff that won't stay on the job long, you'll just have to do the work again soon. A low-durability compound wastes your time and money.

2. Shrinkage. Does the caulk shrivel after application? The answer to that one may not matter much if you're planning on caulking crevices less than $\frac{1}{16}$ inch wide or some inside corners (where two wings of a house meet, for example). Shrunken caulk in an inside corner actually looks less obtrusive than a fat bead; shriveled compound in the skinny cracks will be hardly noticed. High-shrinkage caulk in crannies wider than $\frac{1}{16}$ inch, however, will form concavities that cast shadows and attract dirt.

3. *Ease of application.* This is an especially important item if you have a lot of caulking to do. Who wants to spend hours working with a caulk that flows unevenly from the cartridge or refuses to be easily tooled?

4. *Paintability.* Most caulks last longer if you paint them after application. And without a coat or two, many compounds will collect dirt or darken with age. So to be on the safe side, check the label for painting information—and stick with the paintables.

5. *Versatility.* Different compounds are good for different surfaces and cracks. Some caulks work better on metal-to-masonry joints than others; some do their best only on crevices no wider than $\frac{1}{2}$ inch; some should be used only on interior surfaces; some do just fine on almost anything. Read the label to be sure.

6. *Safety.* Caulking compounds are *not* as benign as toothpaste. Several of them contain flammable substances; a few can irritate your skin or eyes; some give off harmful vapors or disagreeable odors. Your best protection is a little horse sense. Don't smoke while caulking, keep caulk away from children, wash your hands after application, and respect label precautions.

7. *Cost.* This is the last consideration because it's the least important. All the preceding factors should carry more weight than the price tag.

Now for a rundown on the most popular types of compounds on the market. The following notes should help guide you to the caulking material with the characteristics you want.

Cord or rope caulks. These most often come in the form of strands of oakum (the ancient sailing caulk) or oil-base compound. You stuff the material in cracks wider than $\frac{1}{2}$ inch, often as a base for beads of regular cartridge caulk. It's fairly easy to apply and resists shrinkage well, but it won't last more than 2 years. It costs pennies a foot.

Oil- or resin-base caulks. These are the cheapest compounds you can buy. They are usually regarded as low-durability, high-shrinkage products, but there may be a few of them on the market that can match the performance of more expensive brands. Oil- and resin-base caulks bond to wood, masonry, and metal, but they may harden and crack within 3 years. Some brands need a surface primer; some are difficult to tool or "gun" into cracks. These caulks clean up with paint thinner.

Latex caulks. Like oil- or resin-based caulks, latex caulks have a broad range of durability among the brands. Generally, though, latex compounds outlast the oil- and resin-base ones, and they shrink less, too. They have about the same ease of application. The latex caulks can be used on most surfaces, are cleaned up with soap and water, and are painted to boost longevity. They are a low-cost sealer.

Butyl rubber caulks. Although their range of durability is wide, these compounds generally have the edge over latex. You can find cartridges of butyl with a 10-year warranty. The stuff bonds to most surfaces, usually goes on about as well as the preceding types, and cleans up with naphtha or paint thinner. One big drawback: some brands have high shrinkage. Another inexpensive leak-stopper.

Acrylic latex caulks. As far as durability goes, these compounds are generally neck and neck with butyl rubber. They usually don't shrink as much, though, and many of them go on easier. They bond to most materials and clean up with soap and water. Moderately priced.

Polysulfide caulks. These belong to that revered group of synthetic compounds known as the elastomerics. And like all elastomerics, the polysulfides are expensive and highly durable. Some have 20-year warranties. The polys will bond to just about anything and usually shrink very little, but they may be tough to apply. If you want to use them on porous surfaces, you'll have to lay down a primer first. They may irritate your skin during application, too, and will probably require a special cleaner.

Polyurethane caulks. These are elastomerics, too, and closely match the polysulfides in durability, shrinkage, ease of application, surface versatility, and price. Also like the sulfides, the urethanes require special cleaners and may irritate your skin. They could give off noxious fumes as well. But there is no need for a primer.

Silicone caulks. Silicone caulks are the top-of-the-heap elastomerics. They are generally very durable, very shrink-resistant, very easy to apply, and very expensive. You could spend $6 a cartridge for this compound. You can apply silicones just about anywhere, but you can't paint many of them. And if you can't paint them, they're going to weather faster and maybe pick up dirt. They always require special cleaners and sometimes a primer. Beware of noxious vapors and other hazards.

How to Caulk

A caulking gun, a few cartridges of caulk, and some cord or rope caulk—that's all you need to handle 99% of your weatherization caulking.

But, you say, *how many* cartridges of caulk and *how much* strand caulk? That's easy. You can usually count on a standard cartridge (10 to $11\frac{1}{2}$ ounces) to deliver a $\frac{1}{4}$-inch bead about 25 feet long. That often works out to approximately one-half cartridge per window or door or four cartridges for the foundation sill. And you can figure how much rope or cord you need by measuring the length of all those extra-wide (over $\frac{1}{2}$ inch) cracks.

The first step in any caulking job is to prepare the surface. Scrape old caulk out of the crevices with a putty knife (Figure 4-46), wire-brush the cracks from one end to the other (Figure 4-47), and clean dirt and grease from the area with a solvent (Figure 4-48). Sound like a lot of trouble? It is. But going to the trouble will give your caulk years of extra adhesion.

And don't forget about priming. Some caulks need a primed surface more than others, and their labels should tell you so. To be on the safe side, you can prime all porous areas.

After you've cleaned and primed, if needed, and the surfaces are dry as bone, begin with the rope or cord sealers at the big gaps. Uncoil the strands

Fig. 4-46. The old caulk probably will be cracked and loose, so it should scrape out easily.

Fig. 4-47. The wire brush gets the particles of old caulk that your putty knife misses.

and shove them into the crevices with a putty knife, screwdriver, or your fingers (Figure 4-49). The cord or rope can be your sole defense against the breezes or it can be a base for a solid bead of cartridge caulk.

If you have the right caulk to begin with, achieving those solid beads should be a simple task. Tedious maybe, but simple. It helps to have a dependable caulking gun, steady hands, and a temperature no lower than 45°F. You can probably pick up a serviceable gun for less than $6, and with a little practice your hands should be able to handle it steadily. If the temperature is below 45°F, the compound will get stiff and unruly; work when the day is warmer and you'll fare better. If you *must* lay a few beads in the wrong weather, use two cartridges and alternate them. Caulk with one and leave the other in your warm house, then switch them when the chill starts to interfere with the gunning.

Before loading a cartridge into the gun, you'll want to slice the cartridge's nozzle and puncture the seal at the nozzle's base. With a razor blade or utility knife, cut the nozzle at a 45 degree angle, making sure that the

Fig. 4-48. Moisten a rag in solvent and rub away any remaining grease or dirt.

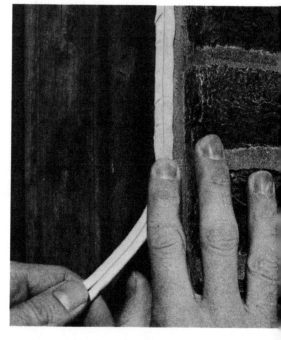

Fig. 4-49. Regardless of how you get this kind of caulk into place, you have to be sure to span the crack completely.

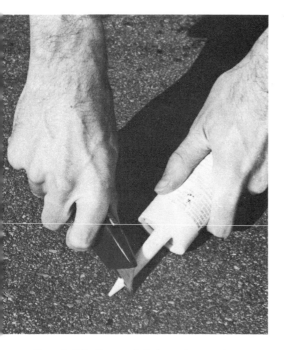

Fig. 4-50. For safety's sake, cut *away* from you, not towards you.

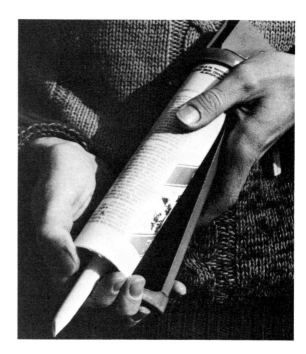

Fig. 4-51. Drop the butt in first, nozzle second.

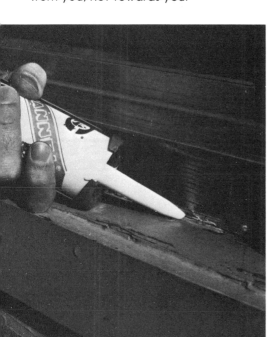

Fig. 4-52. The angle will help you see what's going on and make it easier to modulate the caulk flow.

Fig. 4-53. Don't be afraid of putting on too much caulk; you can smooth out excess later. A bigger problem is not applying enough.

Fig. 4-54. This smoothing job can make your caulk easier to paint.

Fig. 4-55. For long-term storage, plug the tip with a nail and wrap with foil. When you leave the nozzle uncovered, the caulk drys out fast.

diameter of the nozzle is about equal to the width of the crevices you want to fill (Figure 4-50). That angle will give you a little more control over the ribbons you lay. With a long nail pierce the seal so the caulk can flow out evenly.

Then load up. Twist the gun's plunger so its teeth disengage from the trigger, pull the plunger all the way back, and drop a cartridge into the barrel (Figure 4-51). Rotate the plunger again so the teeth are ready to bite, shove it forward until they engage the trigger, and you're all set.

To begin caulking, hold the gun at a 45 degree angle and slip the nozzle into the crack (Figure 4-52). Pull the trigger to start the caulk oozing and slide the nozzle down the joint, drawing an even bead that "grips" both sides of the crevice (Figure 4-53). It may take you awhile to coordinate the trigger-pulling and the nozzle-moving for a smooth ribbon, but you'll get the hang of it. Just be sure to fill every crack completely. That means filling the deep ones from the bottom up. When you get to the end of your run, twist the plunger to disengage it. If you don't, the pressure in the gun will keep pushing caulk out the nozzle even after you've released the trigger.

If you like, you can smooth out the caulk beads by running a wet finger or ice cream stick along them (Figure 4-54). If caulk ends up on a surface where it shouldn't be, clean up the mess fast with a cloth soaked in water or an appropriate solvent.

After the job's done, you'll want to save any caulk that's left. Just stick a 10-penny nail in the nozzle hole and wrap the nozzle in aluminum foil (Figure 4-55).

CHAPTER FIVE

Windows and Doors:
Slowing the Energy Drain

AS necessary as they are, windows and doors are really just holes in the walls, plugged by materials that never did and never will get high scores for insulating efficiency. If you worked through the calculations in chapter 2, you may have found out that your windows squander twenty times as much heat as equal areas of insulated wall; your doors, seven times as much. And all those Btu's that slowly seep away can put an enormous strain on your budget, perhaps to the tune of $500 a year.

So how do you slash those costs? Ten years ago the answer was "storm windows and doors!" But a new day has dawned, and there are a lot of new ideas for trimming window and door heat losses. Now there are insulating shutters, thermal shades, foam-core doors, and more. This chapter is a review of those options, a guide to the weaknesses and strengths of worthy insulating technologies. Take a close look at the possibilities, from conventional storm windows and doors to the latest "movable insulation," and then decide what's right for the holes in your walls. And don't be shy about putting *any* option to the critical test—the cost-effectiveness analysis of chapter 2.

STORM WINDOWS, TRADITIONAL AND MODERN

In chapter 1 you learned that a sheet of glass is a rotten insulator, with an R-value of a mere 0.88. That means that a single-pane window stops heat flow about as well as a sieve stops water. A storm window provides an extra layer of glazing for extra protection. The additional layer and the air space it creates can reduce conduction by 50%, and the overall seal can put a respectable dent in infiltration losses. That kind of conservation means a savings on your heating bill *and* your air conditioning costs.

Storm windows can also act as solar collectors, gathering in free radiant heat from the sun. In sunny times, a south-facing single-pane window will gain about as much radiant heat during the day as it loses at night. But with south-facing storm windows, the sunshine beams through but has trouble radiating back out because of the dual glazing. The result is a net gain in heat. Btu's free of charge. However, this kind of ray-collecting will work for your storms (or any other multiple-glazing configuration) only when (1) at least half your winter days are sunny and (2) your "collectors" are facing southward. Cloudy days do you no good, and windows facing north, east, or west don't get enough sun exposure to be useful heat collectors. This last point is nice to know if you can afford to install storms on only a few windows a season and you're wondering which ones to do first. Obviously, your top priority is the windows facing south.

So there's something to gain by putting storms on all your windows, but let's keep a proper perspective. Though a storm window can cut heat losses in half and siphon off some sun, it still nudges a single-pane's R-value to only about 2. Compared to the R-value of most walls, that's downright trifling. It's better than 0.88, but it's still way too low. And this is why a few experts have begun to question the usefulness of storms, especially since these weatherizers are relatively expensive. So know the score before you invest. Storm windows may be the perfect weatherization option for certain windows, but compared to all the new window insulators out there, storms have a lousy conservation record.

Basically there are only three categories of storm windows: conventional single-panes, conventional combinations (double- and triple-track), and single-pane kits. For the most part, they are intended for use with double-hung windows, America's favorite kind, so the discussion below is geared for them. But you can now buy storms that are specially made for casements and sliders. Your glass dealer is the one to ask.

Conventional Single-Panes

The conventional single-pane storm windows are simply metal-framed sheets of glass or rigid plastic that you fasten to the outside of your windows (Figure 5-1). You usually hang or attach them in some way so you can

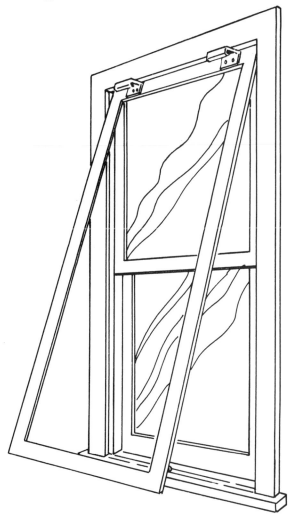

Fig. 5-1. A conventional single-
pain storm window with mounting brackets.

remove them easily at end of season. They don't open, of course, so you have
to install them with a careful eye to fire escape routes. If you have air conditioning, you might want to leave these storms up year round, for they
fight heat gain as well as heat loss. If you do not have air conditioning,
you'll probably install them just before winter and take them down just
after.

For around $20 to $40 you can get one of these single-pane types from
a storm window supplier, probably not as a stock item, but as a custom-made
unit built to your specifications. You give the supplier the height and width

of the windows you plan to cover and he either sends your order off to be filled or builds the windows himself. Whatever the procedure is, you'll want to carefully check the storms he sells you. Don't accept anything that doesn't match your order. Furthermore, look for the features that make storms durable: heavy-gauge metal frames, anodized or baked enamel frame finishes, frame corner joints that are solid, fasteners and other hardware that can withstand years of weathering, and airtight seams between the glazing and frame. It never hurts to shop around for storms with all the right ingredients.

There is nothing difficult about putting up these weatherizers. It is usually just a matter of fastening them to your primary window exteriors with screws, or attaching metal brackets at the tops of your windows so the single-panes can hang in place. At any rate, installation procedures can vary from storm to storm, so always consult your supplier.

Combination Types

Conventional combination storm windows are different creatures altogether, though they do the same basic job as the single-panes and just as effectively. They're the most popular storm windows in the nation, basically because they're so convenient. In the case of the triple-track combinations (the best-selling kind), you *permanently* install them on your window exteriors and open them when you please. No annual installation and take-down. No worries about fire exit routes. Figure 5-2 shows how all this convenience comes about. There are two sashes and a screen, all of which move in grooves, or tracks, in the frame. In winter you raise one sash, lower the other, and let the resulting barrier fight off the freeze. You can remove the screen from its track or leave it in year round. When summer comes along, you can raise or lower one of the sashes to let in a breeze while the screen keeps out the bugs. And when you want to clean the window, you can remove the sashes just as you would the screen.

There's a double-track version, too, with one groove for a screen, another for a sash. The system is permanently attached to the outside of your window, as is the triple-track version. You slide the sash into the track for winter and, if you prefer, out of the track for summer. You can leave the screen in or out as you like.

Although there are only two different kinds of combination storm windows to choose from, shopping for the right double or triple is not necessarily a piece of cake. Some combination storms have plastic frames; some

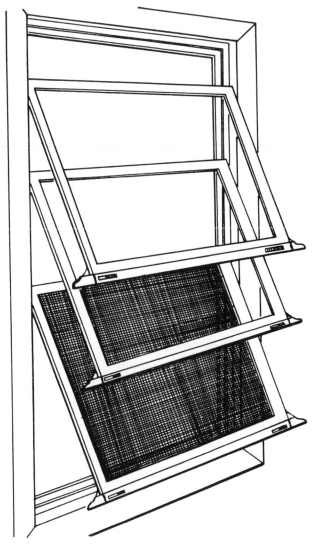

Fig. 5-2. A typical triple-track combination storm window.

have aluminum ones. Some have plastic glazing; some, regular glass. Some are made better than others. And, of course, prices vary widely—$24 to $100 per window. So shop around. Look for sturdy frames with sides that don't bow away from the sashes, frames with "tie bars" that keep the frame sides in alignment. Ask about tracks that have "anti-bow pins" to help the sashes fit tightly in the grooves. Insist on weatherstripping around the sashes. Prefer the combinations that have sashes that lock fast. Ignore the combos with sashes that wobble in the locked position when you touch them. And make sure that the storms you buy have "weep holes" in their frames. Those tiny openings let condensation run off, but they also allow rain that gets through the screen to drain away from the woodwork.

When you think about installation, ask yourself whether you're willing to pay the $24 to $100 per window and install the storms yourself *or* pay 10 to 15% more to have your supplier do the work. If you decide on the do-it-yourself approach, you'll have to measure each one of your primary windows, give the measurements to your supplier, ensure that he fills the order according to your specs, nail or screw the storms to your window exteriors, and caulk around each unit. Your supplier can give you instructions. It's straightforward work—but time consuming.

If you want your supplier to handle the installation *he'll* have to do all the measuring. Once he shows up at your place with your storms, it shouldn't take him more than a day to install them all. But beware. Hiring out this kind of work can be tricky. To cut your risks, deal only with a reputable, experienced installer. *And get it all in writing.* Insist on a contract that spells out *exactly* what kind of storms you're getting—the size, the brand, the color, the weatherstripping. Be sure that you've got the terms of payment right there in black and white. And don't sign the contract unless it specifies a warranty on both installation and storms. After you get your contract and the work is ready to commence, conduct an inspection. Make sure that the storms that come in on the truck are the ones you ordered. And after the work is all over, inspect again. Demand that the job meets your specifications. If the sashes don't glide smoothly in the tracks and seal when closed, tell the installer. You don't have to accept substandard workmanship.

Interior Single-Pane Kits

If you have more faith in your own workmanship than someone else's, maybe you should look into the last category of storm windows, the single-pane kits. They're the *real* news in residential storm windows. They're inexpensive (around $7 to $23 apiece), usually as effective as conventional storms, about as easy to install as living room curtains, and are a do-it-yourselfer's dream.

The typical kit contains a sheet of glazing (usually acrylic, polyethylene vinyl, polyester, or glass), several framing strips (generally aluminum or plastic), and some means for attaching the storm to the window (most often screws or adhesive). You can probably put all the pieces together and fasten them in place in less than 20 minutes. You may have to trim the glazing or framing strips to size, but that's a simple job. And chances are, the whole thing will go on the *inside* of your window, away from the elements. There are good exterior kits around, but they can be harder to install than the insiders, and they take an awful beating from Mother Nature, too.

There are several kinds of interior kits: rigid glazing types with aluminum or plastic frames (Figures 5-3 and 5-4), the plastic film versions also with aluminum or plastic frames (Figure 5-5), and some film kinds with no frames at all (Figure 5-6). As far as energy saving is concerned, there isn't much difference among them. If they're installed correctly, they're all going to do a decent job of cutting heat loss, fighting infiltration, and providing R-values comparable to those of conventional storm windows. It's hard to say which type will last longest, though it's a safe bet the vinyl films will wear out faster than most of the other glazings. These films can also distort the view through them, which is something to consider before you buy.

To install the rigid glazing kits you usually have to hacksaw or scissors-cut the framing strips to match your window size, sometimes slice the glazing to fit in the frame, and generally attach the customized sash to your window trim with screws or self-adhesive. It's much the same with the plastic-film-and-frame kits, except that you have to stretch the floppy glazing across the frame, inserting it in grooves that allow you to pull the film taut as a drum.

The no-frame kits offer you the most straightforward installation of all. Just cut the film to your window size and tape it to your window trim. With the right kind of weatherstripping tape, this film sash will give you an airtight seal. But, of course, you don't have to buy a kit to get all the makings for such a storm. You can simply buy yourself a roll of 6-mil polyethelene sheeting and some weatherstripping tape and go to it. Regardless of how you buy the pieces, there can be no doubt that a film-and-tape storm is the cheapest there is.

Exterior Kits

The exterior kits are not nearly as popular as interior varieties. Maybe it's because installing the exteriors often means climbing ladders and craning your neck, or maybe it's because there are only a few exterior kit types around.

Fig. 5-3. This rigid-glazing insider storm pane has hinges to allow for easy access to the primary window. (Courtesy Plaskolite, Inc.)

Fig. 5-4. This rigid insider storm pane sports crystal-clear plastic glazing and self-adhesive mounting trim. (Courtesy Plaskolite, Inc.)

Fig. 5-5. Here's a framed-film kit that features clear vinyl sheeting and self-adhesive snap-apart molding. (Courtesy Plaskolite, Inc.)

Fig. 5-6. The no-frame kit is basically just a sheet of plastic film that you tape over your window. (Courtesy Plaskolite, Inc.)

The rigid glazing versions with aluminum or plastic frames look a whole lot like the rigid glazing insiders and have comparable R-values. The glazing is usually acrylic, but you may happen upon other types of sheeting. These outsider kits are often installed by simply pressing the self-adhesive frames to the exterior window trim. There are a few types around that come with pivoting clasps that hold the storm frames to your windows' outer woodwork. Either way, you'll get the performance you want—but not for as long as you might like. The weather will give these outsiders a thrashing and cut big chunks out of their lifespans.

If you look hard enough, you'll be able to find an exterior version of the interior no-frame kit. Instead of tape, though, most kits come with cardboard strips that you place around the edges of the plastic film and staple or tack to the perimeter of your window. Of course, there's nothing stopping you from bypassing the kit route and buying your own polyethylene and accessories separately.

Just one final note about storm kits, a note saved for last because of its importance: nearly every storm kit on the market is a slight fire hazard when installed. Most kits will burn when exposed to flames, just as most drapes will. And many kit sashes can't be opened easily after installation, which could be a big problem in a house fire. This news shouldn't keep you from considering the kits—just be well aware of the potential hazard.

PULLING THE SHADES ON HEAT LOSS

Take an ordinary vinyl window shade and replace the skinny roller up top with an outsized one designed to accommodate a lot of shade material. Then add some insulating power to the vinyl: laminate on a layer of fiber batting, some reflective foil, and some heavy decorative cloth. What do you have? A thermal rollup shade.

Ever since the recent revolution in window insulators (called "movable insulation"), a huge assortment of thermal rollups have hit the market, not to mention thermal shutters and other window energy-savers. These new shades and shutters offer R-values that beat out storm windows every time—from about 1.5 to as much as 14.0. That means that for the first time since the invention of our glorified holes-in-the-wall, we've got a chance to make them energy-efficient. And because the cost of the movables is comparable to that of storms, they're bound to be more cost-effective.

"Movable" implies that some homeowner muscle is involved. And there's the rub. Unlike storm windows that stay put to do their jobs yet let you look out on the world, thermal rollup shades and other movables require a lot of attention. To let the sun in during the day, you'd probably want to raise the shades, especially those on south-facing windows. But every winter night you want to lower the shades to trap the heat inside your house. Not everyone is willing to go around raising and lowering their shades morning and night, not even for giant cuts in heat loss.

"Blanket" Shades

But if you are willing to be an active shade manager, you've got a lot of options to choose from. Perhaps the simplest ones are those that consist of thick blankets of plastic or fiber, like the hypothetical makeshift unit I described. A good example of this kind is the Window Quilt system from Appropriate Technology Corporation (Figure 5-7). The shade material is a multi-layered fabric of polyester fiberfill, aluminized plastic film, and polyester blend covers, all quilted together in a decorative pattern. The fiberfill and the covers slow down conduction, and the aluminized plastic reflects radiant heat and stops the passage of moisture. Like all good thermal shades, the Window Quilt seals on all sides. A double roller configuration keeps the shade pressed tightly against the top of the window; tracks mounted on the sides of the window firmly grip the edges of the shade; and a weighted batten along the shade bottom pushes its foam-rubber strip securely against the sill.

The manufacturer claims that the Window Quilt system gives you an R-value of 3.4, but *Consumer Reports* says that you should expect only about 2.5. Whatever the value is, you can be sure it's a world better than the R = 1 for storm windows. And the all-around-the-window seal reduces infiltration in a big way.

One of the key selling points of the Window Quilt is good looks. No, movable insulation doesn't have to be ugly. Most of the thermal shades on the market are at least as attractive as ordinary shades. And, as you can see, some of the thermals may be better looking than many curtains. A few heat-stopping shades even come in different colors.

Other Thermal Rollups

Another type of thermal rollup shade uses trapped air as its big insulator. Usually the shade consists of several layers of plastic film which separate when the shade is rolled down to create pockets of air. One such shade is the Independence 10 by Independent Systems Corporation (Figures 5-8 and 5-9). It's made of an inner loop of metallized Mylar encased in a larger

Fig. 5-7. This attractive Window Quilt unit offers a decorative outer surface, several insulating layers, and an air seal on all sides. (Courtesy Appropriate Technology Corporation)

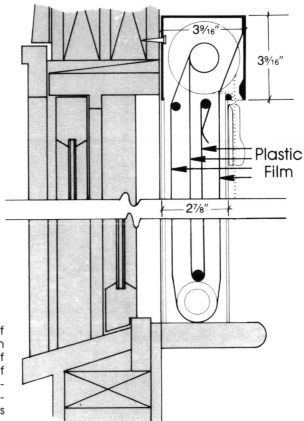

Fig. 5-8. In this cross-section of the Independence 10 you can see how the insulating layers of dead air between sheets of plastic film are built into the special rollup configuration. (Courtesy Independent Systems Corporation)

outer loop of opaque vinyl film. This loop-within-a-loop creates three heat-retarding air chambers when you roll down the shade. The shade material rests snugly inside a frame that you attach to the sides and top of your window. When you lower the shade, your window takes on the look of a solid wall; raise the shade and it retracts into a roll at the top of the window. And, believe it or not, the manufacturer touts an R-value of 10.71.

Other thermal rollups are made of single sheets of aluminized plastic film, of interlocking hollow slats that raise and lower like the slats of a roll-top desk, or of vinyl film with a metallized plastic face. The market is expanding, so you may find yet other styles.

Before You Buy

In spite of the diversity of thermal shades available, there are a few generalizations that may be helpful when you set out to buy the perfect shade.

Fig. 5-9. This is how the Independence 10 might look on your window. Only the shade material shows; no rollers or mechanism are visible. (Courtesy Independent Systems Corporation)

First, expect to pay about $2 to $6 a square foot for thermal shades, no matter what kind you select. That comes to about $90 per shade for some brands, about what you'd pay for a good combination storm window. But remember that energy-saving shades will pay for themselves a great deal faster than storms will. Second, if you want valance boxes or other shade accessories, you'll probably have to build your own or buy them as extras. It's easy enough, though, to surround most thermal shades with curtains. Third, installation is complicated and time consuming. The average do-it-yourselfer can handle it, all right, but it may take 6 to 8 hours per shade. Every manufacturer has its own set of instructions, and some of them are clearer than others. Fourth, you usually can't go right out and buy your favorite shade. Chances are, you'll first have to send away to the manufacturer for information regarding their product. Some companies even have special instructions for measuring your windows. After you find out what you need to know and measure everything, you'll probably have to mail your order in to the manufacturer. They'll make up your order and ship it to your house. *Then* you start installing.

Here are a few of the manufacturers, waiting for your inquiry. Keep in mind, though, that company addresses and product lines are subject to change.

> Appropriate Technology Corporation
> PO Box 975
> Brattleboro, VT 05301
> Independent Systems Corporation
> PO Box 329
> Airline Park
> Durham, CT 06422
> Joel Berman Associates, Inc.
> 102 Prince Street
> New York, NY 10012
> Plastic-View Transparent Shade, Inc.
> PO Box 25
> Van Nuys, CA 91408
> Solar Energy Components, Inc.
> 212 Welsh Pool Road
> Lionville, PA 19353
> Solar Energy Construction Company
> Box 718
> Valley Forge, PA 19481
> Wind-N-Sun Shield, Inc.
> PO Box 2504
> Indian Harbor Beach, FL 32937
> Sun Control Products, Inc.
> 431 Fourth Avenue, SE
> Rochester, MN 55901

CLOSING THE SHUTTERS ON ENERGY WASTE

Most exterior shutters dress up your windows and sometimes keep high winds from smashing the glass, but they're usually not much on saving energy. The new interior thermal types, however, are supposed to have more than just pretty faces—they're designed to give you handsome energy savings, too. In fact, today's buy-and-put-together thermal shutters offer you R-values of 2.5 to 9.1. Most of them look and operate like conventional shutters but insulate like no conventional shutter ever made. The only serious drawback is price. They can cost from $2.25 to $16.00 per square foot, or about $35 to $240 per shutter, plus shipping. And that doesn't include any decorative coverings or finishes you might want to buy to enhance their looks.

Most of the energy-saving shutters have a lot in common, at least on the outside. Most of them have a bifold configuration, hinge to the sides of your windows, weight about 18 to 45 pounds, seal tightly around your window perimeters, and interfere with curtains and drapes when they fold up. But what's on the inside is what really counts, and that's where most of the design diversity is. Some shutter cores are mostly dead air; others, rigid foam insulation; a few have both air and foam. And the ingredients can be tossed together in countless ways.

Fig. 5-10. The bifold InsulShutter offers a wood-grain exterior that conceals a heat-stopping core. (Courtesy InsulShutter, Inc.)

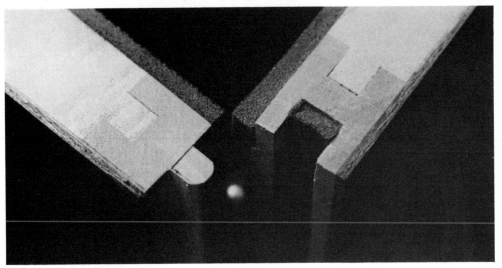

Fig. 5-11. This construction ensures minimal air seepage where the shutter sections join. (Courtesy InsulShutter, Inc.)

Commercial Thermal Shutters

An interesting example of the foam-core type is the InsulShutter by InsulShutter, Inc. (Figure 5-10). The guts of it is a $\frac{3}{4}$-inch insulating board (polyisocyanurate) sandwiched between layers of reflective foil and plywood panels. The shutter sections fit inside a wooden frame and sport metal hardware (hinges, sash lock, and perimeter spring lock) just like any conventional shutter. To reduce infiltration around each section, there is polyurethane weatherstripping along all the joints, even in the tongue-and-groove channels where the sections meet (Figure 5-11). Its ability to stop air seepage is first rate. All this material weighs in at a hefty 40 pounds and delivers an R of 9.1 (according to the manufacturer) or 4.5 (according to *Consumer Reports*).

Another shutter fairly representative of the field is the SunSaver by Homesworth Corporation (Figure 5-12). It's a dead-air type with two sheets of Thermoply (insulating cardboard) enclosing a $\frac{3}{4}$-inch air space, all framed out with wood. The outer surface of each Thermoply sheet is white for a neat appearance, and the inner surface is aluminized to reflect heat. The system comes with hinges, knobs, and other accoutrements. And as with any other thermal shutter, you can spruce up the outer surfaces as you please with the fabric or veneer of your choice (Figure 5-13). The whole thing

Fig. 5-12. This is the "double door" SunSaver shutter by Homesworth. They make a bifold version, too. (Courtesy Homesworth Corporation)

weighs 18 pounds, costs around $30 including shipping, and slashes heat loss with an R-value of 4.42 (manufacturer) or 4.50 *(Consumer Reports)*. It does a fine job of beating infiltration, too.

Nearly everything I said about using, ordering, and installing thermal shades applies to these heat-saving shutters, as well. Certainly these shutters require vigilance to open and close them at the right times. Surely it will take some elbow grease to attach them to your windows (4 or 6 hours per shutter). And inevitably you'll have to send away to the manufacturer for information before you place your order by mail. Here are names and addresses of some professional shutter-makers:

    FTR
      5725 Arapahoe
      Boulder, CO 80303
    Homesworth Corporation
      18 Main Street
      Yarmouth, ME 04096

InsulShutter, Inc.
  110 North Seventh Street
  Silt, CO 81652
Wallrich, Inc.
  2601 E. Missouri
  El Paso, TX 79903

Easy Pop-In Shutters

Of course, you could build your own insulating shutters from scratch. The job isn't really as tough as it sounds, and there's at least one gadget that simplifies the project considerably. It's the Nightwall Clip produced by Zomeworks Corporation. It's nothing more than a 3- or 6-inch magnetic strip and an accompanying steel counterpart that helps you fasten a sheet of rigid foam insulation to your window. Pick up a few sheets of polystyrene

Fig. 5-13. The SunSaver, all dressed up with patterned fabric. (Courtesy Homesworth Corporation)

at your lumberyard (the 1-inch-thick stuff will do), cut them to fit in the sashes (next to the glazing), attach the magnetic strips around the window at 2-foot intervals, attach the steel mates to corresponding positions on the foam boards, and just slip the insulation into position. The clips will keep the board $\frac{3}{32}$ inch from the glazing, virtually eliminating convection currents. And the foam is bound to give you healthy R-values to halt conduction, maybe as high as 4 or 5. The clips will be hardly noticeable, and you can slap on any panel covering you want, or conceal your makeshift shutters with your curtains. Just one drawback: because these heat shields are "pop-in" shutters, very unlike the hinged kind, you'll have to find a place to store them during the sunny hours. The cost for such custom-built shutters will be about $7 for a minimum order of twenty 3-inch clips, $10 for a minimum order of 6-inch clips, and 35¢ to 60¢ per square foot for 1-inch-thick polystyrene from a lumberyard. Here's the address:

> Zomeworks Corporation
>   Box 712, Dept. OG
>   Albuquerque, NM 87103

Scratch-Built Bifold Shutters

If you're thinking you could get by without Nightwall Clips, you're right. It wouldn't take much to cook up your own panel fasteners or even to hatch your own bifold shutter system. All you'd need for that is a bright idea and a little do-it-youself ingenuity. Assuming you've got all the ingenuity required, a design idea is shown in Figure 5-14. It's a fast-build model, but it's effective—and you can tinker with the design all you want.

Some 1-x-2's, a sheet of $\frac{3}{4}$-inch-thick rigid insulation, a few pieces of $\frac{1}{2}$-inch quarter-round molding, a piece of fabric for covering, some 3-penny finishing nails, a little glue, and some cabinet hardware—these are the makings of our home-grown shutter. You can probably assemble all the parts and attach the whole works to your window in less than 5 hours, about the time it would take you to install a factory-ordered model.

Begin by sawing the 1-x-2's for a frame that will fit tightly inside your window. Your shutters will stay in place with a friction fit, so be sure you size the frame correctly. Then cut eight lengths of quarter-round molding and nail them to the inside edges of the framing pieces. The molding will hold the rigid foam inside the frame, the way a grooved track holds the glazing of a window sash. Because the 1-x-2's are actually only $\frac{3}{4}$ by $1\frac{5}{8}$ inches,

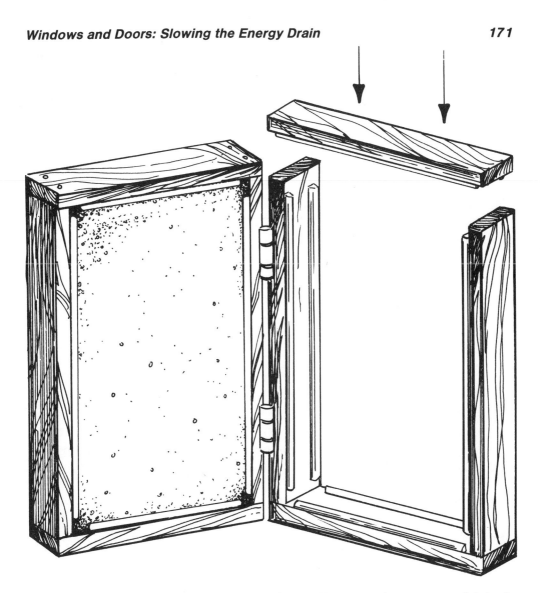

Fig. 5-14. An easy-to-build homemade bifold shutter—a system you can fabricate and install in a single afternoon.

and the quarter-rounds are $\frac{1}{2}$ inch thick, the grooves you get ought to be the perfect width for that $\frac{3}{4}$-inch thick insulation. You'll have to compress the edges of the insulation board a bit to get it in the slots, but that's just fine. The tighter the better.

After the molding's in place, sand and finish all the wood. Then slice the rigid foam to fit inside the frame and glue the fabric to one side of the insulation. Use burlap or satin or denim or your heart's desire—anything goes as long as you're happy with it. While the adhesive is drying, nail and glue the framing pieces together, leaving off one side of the framing so you can slide in the insulation. Slide the foam in place and nail down the last part of the frame. Countersink the nails, touch up the nail holes, attach the hinges and knob, and you're done.

Departures from this design are myriad. Instead of the bifold construction, you can build yourself a pop-in. Or skip the quarter-rounds and cut grooves in the framing pieces to hold the insulation. Or cover both sides of the rigid foam with cardboard or wallpaper or veneer or reflective foil. Or rabbet the frame corners to provide stronger joints. Or build two sets of frames and use them to sandwich in a few layers of Mylar or Thermoply. Or keep right on dreaming until you come up with the idea that tops them all.

DOORS TO ENERGY EFFICIENCY

I bear sad tidings about standard storm doors: they're almost never cost-effective. From an energy standpoint, they're white elephants. If you bought a brand-spanking-new one today, you might not get your money back for 35 years! That's one long payback period. Part of the problem is that most standard doors are relatively energy efficient compared to regular house windows. A conventional window pane has an R-value of about 0.88, but a 2-inch-thick wood exterior door chalks up an R of about 2.33. So right off the bat, storm doors have to work extra hard to save you as much money as storm windows can. And the simple truth is, storm doors usually *can't* work extra hard. Doors are forever flapping in the breeze, and that's how most of the heat-wasting happens. Plus, storm doors generally don't seal tightly because of all that swinging open and shut. They may slow the weathering of your exterior doors; they may provide you with bug screens in summertime; they may make your house look 5 years younger, but conventional storm doors can waste your money. On the other hand, weatherstripping won't waste your money. It's the least you can do for your outer doors.

Foam-Core Doors

If you're serious about pushing your doors' R-values above a 2 or 3, you might want to go a step further than weatherstripping. Get some new doors. Right now you can go out and buy yourself a door that could give you an R as big as 15. It's called a foam-core steel door, and it may be just what the doctor ordered, even if your old doors are still in decent shape. As the name suggests, the door consists of a steel shell filled with foam insulation, and it comes with effective weatherstripping, too. As far as I know, it has only two disadvantages: price (over $150 each) and a tendency to absorb a lot of solar heat. For some homeowners, the big price tag makes the foam-core a poor investment; for others, the door means substantial savings, with a payback of well under 10 years. You'll have to do some chapter 2-type calculations

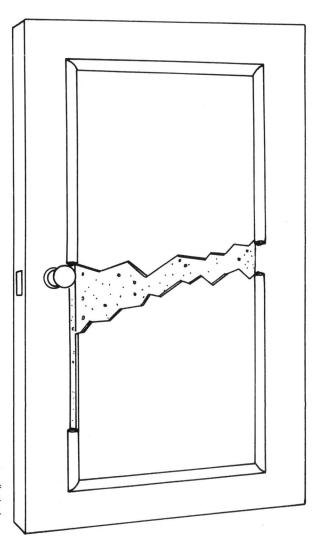

Fig. 5-15. The do-it-yourself insulated door is the perfect substitute for a high-ticket replacement door.

to see if the door is cost-effective for you. The solar heat drawback is an important consideration if the door faces south or west; it can get awfully hot when the sun hits it. In fact, you shouldn't pair one of these with a storm door because the heat buildup between them can be excessive.

You can install a foam-core door yourself or hire a professional to do the work. If you want to go it alone, you may have to choose between hanging just a new door or a new door-frame-and-hardware (called a prehung door). The former is a breeze, but the latter requires advanced handyman skills. Putting in a prehung door means removing your old door plus its casing and hardware, and then nailing and caulking the new door system into the old frame.

The Do-It-Yourself Alternative

If you don't want a new door, you can still give your old door new insulating power. Several years ago another homeowner manual suggested a way to do that, and it's certainly worth trying. Simply add a layer of rigid foam insulation to your door's exterior surface. Glue on a sheet of foam (on the center of the door, away from the hardware), cover the insulation with a thin layer of hardboard (for protection against the elements), and trim the edges of the foam with quarter-round molding (Figure 5-15). Use about any thickness of rigid foam you can get your hands on— $\frac{1}{2}$-inch, $\frac{3}{4}$-inch, 1-inch, whatever. You end up with a door R-value as high as 8 and a raised-panel effect on the door's surface.

And surely one good idea will lead you to another. You may want to add a sheet of reflective foil between the door and the foam to help reflect heat back into your house. Or you could experiment with dead air by sandwiching some of it between two thin layers of insulation, or offsetting the hardboard a bit from the foam. Or you could forego regular rigid foam altogether and use Thermoply. Or you can come up with your own variations.

Patio Doors

Beware of the infamous Btu-waster known as the glass patio door. I save this note for last because glass patio doors are the worst door energy problem you'll ever have. They can throw away heat sixteen times faster than equal areas of walls and conventional doors. The most effective solution to the problem is to treat your glass doors like windows and cover them with thermal shades or shutters. Some of the same companies that make this movable insulation for windows also make it for patio doors.

CHAPTER SIX

Heating and Cooling: Cutting the Cost of Staying Comfortable

DO you remember the bucket analogy in chapter 1? I likened your house to a pail full of holes, one that could leak water nearly as fast as you could pour it in. The point, of course, was that the more heat-seeping gaps you plugged, the less heat you'd have to pump into your house (or out of your house in the summertime). And as we discovered, there are plenty of ways to bucket-patch. Insulation, weatherstripping, door and window strategies—every little bit helps. But sealing up the bucket is just half the picture. The other half involves tinkering directly with the heating system that tries so hard to keep the bucket full. Modify, supplement, replace, or adjust your heating or cooling system and you're bound to save energy dollars. Probably a *lot* of energy dollars. Let's see what can be done.

CONVENTIONAL (CENTRAL) HEATING: MAKING IT WORK

Your central heating system may be one of the biggest wasters of heat dollars in your house. Far too many systems burn at only 50% efficiency or less, even after the serviceman tunes them up. That means that despite proper maintenance, these units send half of their fuel's heat right up the flue. Unfortunately, modifying these heat-wasters may be like patching holes in a sinking ship. The sad truth is that many furnaces and boilers, especially those that are 10 years old or older, aren't worth repairing or upgrading. It's often better in the long run to start fresh with a brand-new high-efficiency system. There have been dramatic innovations in home heating in the last few years, and one of those new-fangled systems just might save you more money than a ton of repairs and modifications to the old clunker.

If your present oil heating plant is over the hill, consider a new oil system with a flame-retention burner. Such a burner mixes oil and air better than standard burners, and can therefore achieve combustion efficiencies of 80 to 85%. Under the best of conditions, standard burners have efficiencies of only 60 to 80%. Or, if you have gas heat, be sure to investigate new gas units with the novel pulse-combustion burners that boast efficiency ratings of 95%. Or look into the not-so-conventional heat pumps, the heater/air conditioners with efficiencies of over 100% in some cases. Over 100%? That's right; I'll tell you more about it later on.

To scrutinize any of these options, you'll have to do some homework. Talk to reputable heating-equipment dealers and contractors. Compare notes with other homeowners. Call your utility company. And do all the telltale calculations: how much money a new heating plant will save you, what its payback period is, and—to cover all the bases—how much you can save by sticking with the clunker and upgrading it.

Table 6-1 should help you with your math. It will show you how many energy-dollars you'll save when you jump from a low efficiency to a higher one, whether you get a new system or modify the one you have. (To find the efficiency of your current unit, consult your heating technician.) You'll see that if you go from a dog of a furnace to a system with a rating of 85%, you're going to save a lot of money. And the payback period will be short,

Table 6-1
Dollar Savings Per $100 of Annual Fuel Cost

From Original Efficiency of	To an Increased Efficiency of					
	55%	60%	65%	70%	75%	80%
50%	$9.10	$16.70	$23.10	$28.60	$33.00	$37.50
55%		8.30	15.40	21.50	26.70	31.20
60%			7.70	14.30	20.00	25.00
65%				7.10	13.30	18.80
70%					6.70	12.50
75%						6.30

Source: U.S. Department of Commerce, U.S. Department of Energy, U.S. Environmental Protection Agency.

perhaps as short as 3 years. But if you go from a system sporting a 70% efficiency to one that offers 80%, your savings will be skimpy, and the payback period will be long. In that case, some appropriate modifications to your present system may be in order.

Upgrading by Down-rating

The first change you should consider for an oil or gas unit is down-rating. That's the process of reducing the heating capacity (output) of a system. In chapter 2 you learned the importance of ensuring that your heating plant has enough capacity, but it's just as vital to make sure your Btu-maker doesn't have too much. You see, when your oil or gas unit has too much muscle, it does a lot of stop-and-start cycling. And that wastes fuel. The more efficient heating plant is usually the one that runs long and rests long, not the one that cuts on and off frequently.

But is excessive capacity likely to plague *your* furnace or boiler? Recent field tests reveal that most heating systems are oversized. Indeed, there's a good chance that your unit has as much as *two and one-half* times the heating capacity it needs. How it got that way is a long story, a tale of outmoded design ideas from the cheap-energy era. Our primary concern is to make sure that your oil or gas system has the right output for your house's makeup and climate. You'll recall from chapter 2 that the "right" output is equal to your design heat load plus 10%. When you compare that number with the nominal capacity listed on your unit's specification label, you'll know whether down-rating is worthwhile. Or you can ask your heating specialist to compare your needs with your heating output. Just be sure he knows you're interested in *realistic* figures, not overblown ones.

Don't bother with this exercise if you have an electric resistance heating system. Oversizing them doesn't lower their efficiencies, it just makes them work extra hard. (But if you *buy* an oversized electric unit, you're wasting money, one of the biggest inefficiencies of all.)

The easiest way to muzzle down your oil or gas system is to have your service technician install a smaller burner nozzle or orifice. This simple change will make your heating plant burn longer on less fuel, decreasing the amount of heat that goes up the flue. Annual fuel savings: up to 10%. The only hitch is that some states may not permit the modification, so be sure to check out the rules and regulations *before* installation. Another trick is to have a two-stage burner valve hooked up to your gas system. In mild weather, when you don't need full system capacity, this little gadget reduces the gas flow to the burner by 50%. It can cut as much as 10% off your heating bills. And what about installing an electronic ignition system in place of your gas pilot? Don't bother. This is one modification you can do without. It's a worthy feature on a *new* furnace or boiler, but it's not cost-effective as an addition to an old unit. It saves you 3% on your gas bill, but that's not enough to offset the cost of purchase and installation.

Burner Replacement

Another key modification is burner replacement. The same high-efficiency burners that streamline the workings of new heating plants are available as retrofits for existing systems, and their efficiencies also reach 80 to 95%. Those rates are high in anyone's book—but so is the cost. For one of these burners you'll probably pay $250 to $900 *plus* installation.

If you're wondering whether the new gas burners can turn your oil-monger into a gas user, the answer is yes. And if you're wondering whether such a move would be cost-effective over the long haul, the answer is maybe. Certainly gas is cheaper than oil or electricity right now, and the performance of the high-efficiency gas burners is impressive. But you have to remember that the price of gas is going up, rising faster than the price of electricity. In a short while, there may be no economic reason at all to switch to gas. And a few experts question whether a converted gas system can run as efficiently as a unit originally equipped to use gas. The safest tack is to review Table 6-1, get the facts from knowledgeable professionals, and examine as many other modifications as you can.

Flue Dampers

Another heat-saving possibility is the flue damper. This gizmo can reduce oil bills by as much as 20% or gas bills by as much as 30%. It performs this feat by simply keeping useful Btu's from escaping up the chimney. When your boiler or furnace cycles off, a lot of residual heat continues to waft up the flue. A good flue damper automatically blocks the flue when the system shuts off, forcing much of the leftover heat to stay indoors where it belongs. When your heating unit starts again, the damper opens up to let flue gases escape to the atmosphere. This trick will yield good results on just about any oil system around, and it will do the same for many gas units: those located in heated sectors of the house, those with flue diameters larger than 5 inches, and those that give you steam or hot-water heat.

Most flue dampers are just short sections of flue pipe with a motor-driven damper plate inside (Figure 6-1). The motor hooks into the heating plant's controls so that the damper will flip open before the heating unit fires up and close a few seconds after the heating unit shuts off. The gadget looks like it would be a cinch to install, but it isn't. Flue dampers are sensitive pieces of equipment requiring *professional* installation. If you install one incorrectly, you could foul up your furnace or boiler. Cost including installation: $100 to $500.

You may recall that there was quite a tempest brewing about flue dampers a few years ago. The controversy centered on the all-important issue of safety. The main concern was the possibility that a damper might malfunction and cause a fire or force poisonous flue gases into the house. But the uproar has since died down. There's now an industrywide standard to help ensure that flue dampers have failsafe features, and Underwriters Labora-

Fig. 6-1. Flue Dampers from Flair Manufacturing Corporation: (clockwise from top) the motorized Stack Pack, two 3-inch-diameter stainless steel Thermal Stack Packs, and the 8-inch-diameter cast iron Thermal Stack Pack.

tories (UL) has tested many (if not all) of the dampers on the market. Dampers are indeed reasonably safe if they're installed properly. The best way to stay clear of installation foulups is to consider only those dampers that carry a UL seal or an American Gas Association Laboratories certificate, to deal only with a competent and trustworthy installer, and to have your heating system serviced before damper installation. Once installed, be alert to any unusual odor or smoke near your furnace or boiler.

Low-Cost Strategies

System replacement or retrofit are two ways to reduce those dreaded heating bills, but we musn't overlook the less expensive routes to better heating efficiency. Thank goodness there are low-cost strategies for the homeowner who can't afford a $2000 replacement furnace or a $400 gas burner. And the nice thing is, these strategies are applicable to just about any heating unit, even those with relatively high efficiencies.

System maintenance is an obvious step toward fuel efficiency, but one that gets forgotten time and time again. Remembering it could decrease your fuel consumption by 10%. The first thing to do is call your heating technician and ask him to take care of the maintenance chores that you can't do yourself. If you have an oil-fired system, ask that every year he adjust and clean the burner, set the fuel-to-air ratio for maximum efficiency, inspect for oil leaks, check the electrical connections, clean the heating elements and surfaces, change the oil filters, adjust the dampers and draft regulator, change the burner nozzle, and check the oil pump. If you own a gas-fired unit, see that every 3 years the serviceman checks the operation of the main gas valve, pressure regulator, and safety control valve and adjusts the primary air supply nozzle for proper combustion. If you have a coal-fired system, make sure that at the end of each heating season your technician adjusts and cleans the stoker and burner.

Your serviceman's labor will cost you only a few bucks per visit, and you'll probably get all your money back in fuel savings in a matter of months. If you find a serviceman who does first-class work, sign a service contract with him. For a nominal yearly fee, he'll give your system an annual cleaning and tuneup *and* grant you free labor on repairs he makes during the year.

For your own part, you can get out your owner's manual. It should tell you how to change or clean the air filters, adjust the fan belt on the blower, vacuum dust from the fan or blower blades, oil the motor and blower bearings, bleed air from hot water radiators, oil the inside of coal screws and hoppers to prevent rust, and adjust and clean the house thermostat. Your labor will cost you nothing, but will earn you measurable savings.

Once you get your heating plant in tip-top shape, you should balance your system's distribution of heat. You probably don't want the same amount of warmth in every room, so you want to ensure that your Btu's get pushed around to the right places. For a hot-air system, balancing means toying with the dampers in the ducts and the registers in the rooms. With a hot-water or steam unit, it means adjusting valves in the heating pipes. For an electric system, it means tinkering with the thermostats in each living space.

Begin by stopping the flow of heat to areas that don't deserve it—that unheated bedroom, that seldom-used den. Close the dampers and registers, shut off the valves, turn the thermostats off (or to their lowest setting). Then regulate the Btu's that go everyplace else. The rec room may need little heat because all the activity there will keep everyone from getting cold. The kitchen may require less heat than any other room in the house because of the Btu's given off by the appliances. The upstairs rooms may get all the heat they want from downstairs.

Don't overlook the little things that fight against a balanced system: draperies that block vents, furniture that gets in the way of registers and radiators, thermostats that won't behave. If a thermostat is positioned so it's in direct sunlight much of the time, right above a radiator or vent, next to a drafty picture window, or on a cold outside wall, it's going to be haywire. And if your only thermostat is located in a room that you want to keep cooler than others, you'll have trouble heating the rest of the house properly. The answer to these problems may be to move the thermostat to a better location. That's a job for your service technician.

You should also give some thought to replacing your current thermostat with an energy-efficient type, the automatic timer thermostat (Figure 6-2). It can save you as much as 20% on your heating bills. You choose the daytime and nighttime temperatures, and in precise, robotlike fashion the thermostat automatically, faithfully lowers its temperature setting at night and raises its setting in the morning. Considering the service this device performs, it's extremely cheap: about $25 to $95 per unit. And you can hook one up yourself in minutes, in the same spot occupied by your old thermostat.

Of course, you don't have to have a robot to set back your thermostat.

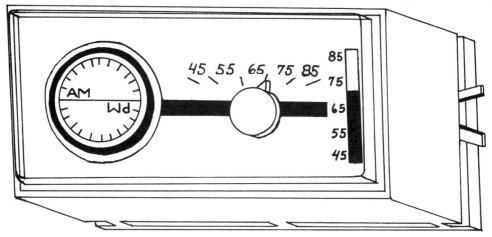

Fig. 6-2. A typical automatic timer thermostat.

You can manually turn back your current thermostat each night and turn it up again in the morning. As long as you're vigilant, you'll save just as much money on the manual plan as you will on the automatic. In fact, no matter how long or how much the setback is, you're going to come out ahead. It's estimated that for every 1°F of round-the-clock setback you'll cut 3% off your heating bill. And for each degree of overnight setback, 1% savings.

I just want to caution you not to try to change the customary temperature in your house too rapidly. If you're used to a room temp of 72°F, a sudden drop to 68°F (the best temperature of most people) will be hard to live with. You have to *slowly* ease into that new way of living, a degree every week or so. And be mindful of the health factor: older people, people with circulatory ailments, or people on certain medications may need higher house temperatures. In these cases, get medical advice.

In chapter 3 I mentioned the importance of insulating heat ducts and pipes that pass through unheated space. There's no better place to re-empha- size that strategy than right here. According to the U.S. Department of Energy, people with well-insulated houses and *un*insulated ducts may be wasting 20 to 40% of their heating plant or air conditioner output. The rem- edy for bare ducts is 2-inch-thick foil-backed insulation. It's cheap but effec- tive. First, caulk any bad duct joints with flexible caulk. Then, surround the ductwork with the insulation (foil side out) and use duct tape to seal any insulation seams and join the insulation sections. As you would expect, the cure for naked pipes is pipe insulation. It too is inexpensive and hard working. You just slip it onto your piping and secure it with duct tape.

AIR CONDITIONING: CUTTING THE COST OF STAYING COOL

Here's a pop quiz. What's the energy efficiency ratio of your room air conditioner or central air unit? And is your system sized correctly? These are the most important conservation questions you can ask about the machine that helps keep you cool. If you don't understand the questions, you may be paying a lot more to cool your house than is necessary. If you know the answers, go to the head of the class.

For those of us stumped by the quiz, let's have a review, starting with question number one. The energy efficiency ratio (EER) of an air conditioner (room or central) is its output (capacity) in Btu's per hour divided by its wattage. That is, the EER is a comparison of how much heat your air conditioner can remove from your house and the amount of energy required to do the removing. For example, a room air conditioner rated at 5000 Btuh with an energy appetite of 800 watts has an EER of 6.25 (5000/800 = 6.25). A second, more efficient model also pegged at 5000 Btuh may run on 600 watts, and therefore offer an EER of 8.33. The larger EER reveals bigger efficiency, and thus points to the more cost-effective machine. The second air conditioner no doubt will cost more than the first. But because the second is about one-third more efficient than the first, and will cost about one-third less to operate, it will save more money in the long run.

The energy efficiency ratio is your best guide to a good buy on an air conditioner. A lot of room air conditioners out there have tags on them telling you the EER's. Today, folks understand that the efficiency of an energy system (which is directly related to operating cost) is often far more significant than the purchase price. So keep an eye open for those tags. If you can't find them, compute the EER's yourself. If the EER is less than 5.0 for a room unit or a whole air system, give a rating of *poor*. If from 5.0 to 7.5, *fair*. If from 7.5 to 10.0, *good*. If above 10.0, *excellent*.

Be sure to check the EER of your existing system. It may be your only proof that your old air conditioner is robbing you blind and your best justification for dumping your old machine and getting a more efficient one. After all, trying to maintain a unit that has outrageous operating costs is like burning dollar bills.

Now about quiz question number two. It asks if your house-cooler has the right capacity for the job at hand. If a furnace or boiler needs to be sized to the right output, then so does an air conditioning unit. Like a heating plant, your air conditioner operates most efficiently when it doesn't have to cycle on and off in spurts. The long-distance run is best. So if you need only about 18,000 Btuh of cooling capacity, your air conditioner should deliver 18,000 Btuh. If your system is way out of line with your needs, you may be better off with a new system.

How do you determine what the proper size air conditioner is? You need to ask a professional. The variables in the size equation are many, including the number of windows in the space to be cooled, the number of heat-emitting appliances involved, the amount of thermal insulation surrounding the living space, the direction the windows face, and more.

Once you've found answers to our two quiz questions, you can move on to other matters, such as energy-saving maintenance. Some people may *think* their air conditioning unit is maintenance-free, but their assumption costs them energy dollars every day. As in furnace or boiler maintenance, taking care of an air conditioning unit means calling in a professional on some things and doing it yourself on others.

Once a year, ask your serviceman to give your central air system a thorough inspection and tuneup. He should check electrical switches and contacts, oil the bearings on fan and compressor if they're not sealed, measure the electrical current drawn by the compressor, flush the evaporator drain line, inspect for refrigerant leaks, check the pulley belt tension, and add refrigerant if necessary. Every 2 months during the season, you can drag out your owner's manual and give your room or central air conditioner a boost by cleaning or replacing the air filter, vaccuuming the condenser and evaporator coils, oiling the fan motor housing if necessary, and straightening any bent coil fins.

As you might expect, many of the Btu-saving measures that work on your heating system can also do wonders for your cooling equipment. Try balancing your system by closing the appropriate doors and floor vents, clearing obstacles away from cooling vents, properly adjusting the dampers in the ducts, and aiming vent louvers upwards. Reduce your cooling load by using your kitchen vent fan to draw out hot air, keeping the sun off room air conditioners or outside compressors, letting attic and window fans pull cool air into the house, turning off heat-generating appliances, using shutters and blinds to reduce solar heat gain, shutting off your air conditioner when you leave the house for more than an hour, insulating the cooling ducts, and raising the thermostat setting to 80°F. This last scheme may reduce your cooling costs by over 50%. To some homeowners, such a reduction can mean an annual savings of at least $100. To others, it can mean much, much more.

THE HEAT PUMP

Here is an extraordinary electrical machine that can pull energy right out of thin air, a device that can extract Btu's from the cold outdoors and transport the heat into your house, a technological marvel that takes little bites of fuel and produces big housefuls of warmth, a system with a split personality, ready to warm you in winter or cool you in summer. Surely the heat pump sounds too good to be true. But it's real, and it comes with all the advantages and disadvantages of a real-world heating/cooling plant. It may cut your annual heating bill by as much as 50%—and disappoint you with its unexpected drawbacks.

How it Works

To understand how these things work, you have to think of them as, well, pumps, not heaters or air conditioners. A heat pump's lot in life is not to *generate* heat like a furnace, but to *gather* heat and *pump* it from one place to another. A heat pump actually absorbs heat from one medium (water or air) and transfers the Btu's to another medium (also water or air). Take a typical air-to-air heat pump, for example. As you can see from Figure 6-3, the system components are all connected by tubing, tubing that loops into coils on both the outdoor and indoor side of the unit. The tubing carries a refrigerant, usually Freon, and it's this stuff that makes possible the transfer of heat from outside to inside your house. When the refrigerant leaves the indoor side, it's a warm liquid. When it hits the expansion valve, it vaporizes, expanding into a gas that's colder than the outdoor air. And when this gas enters the outdoor coil (the evaporator), it sucks up heat from the air passing over the coil. (Yes, there's heat even in the coldest winter air.) From the evaporator, the now warm gas slips into the compressor, where it's crushed into a liquid again—a liquid made hot by the crushing. As this heat-laden liquid reaches the inside coil (the condenser), the Btu's race to the cooler surrounding air inside the house. A fan speeds the released heat on its way. The cycle repeats, and the warmth keeps coming until the outdoor

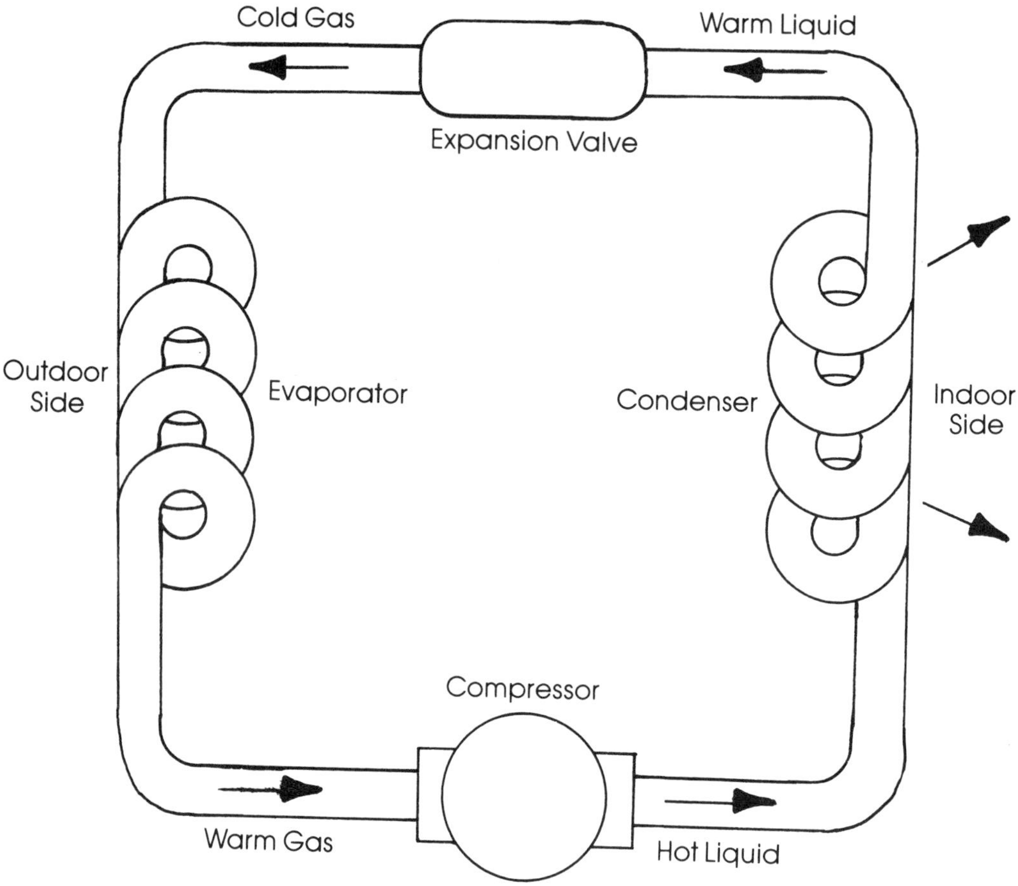

Fig. 6-3. The cycle of an air-to-air heat pump.

temperature drops too low. (More on this in a moment.) In summer the heat pump's reversing valve flops the cycle so you can extract heat from indoors and pump the Btu's outside, just like an air conditioner.

The basic operating principle of this air-to-air unit applies to all other types of heat pumps. The same principle is at work in those systems that move heat from air to water or water to air, those that function as hot water heaters, those that use solar energy, those that hook up to your furnace, and those that are independent enough and small enough to sit on your window sill. Also common to all types are the two factors that every heat pump owner (or potential owner) must confront: balance point and efficiency.

Balance Point

The balance point is the low outdoor temperature I mentioned, the one at which the heat pump has trouble picking up heat. For most heat pumps this is around 20 to 30°F. At the balance point even the stoutest pump can't siphon enough Btu's from the surrounding medium to be truly efficient. Past the balance point is the realm of bad economics. So heat pumps must have help to ride out these low outdoor temperatures, and they get that help in the form of backup heating systems. A common arrangement is the addition of electric resistance heaters built right into the heat pump. They can carry the full heating load when the mercury slips down too far. Another configuration is the heat pump with a conventional heating system as an auxiliary unit. The pump does most of the heating, but falls back on a furnace or boiler when the going gets rough. The pump and the conventional system use the same ducts or pipes and get along just fine.

The implication of all this is clear: heat pumps are most economical in regions with mild winters, places where temperatures below freezing are rare. Above the balance point, the heat pump will out-perform any other heating system. Below the balance point, the pump relies on a conventional heat-maker with conventional efficiency. Of course, if you're paying through the nose for oil or electricity, this kind of performance may save you money no matter where you live.

Efficiency

The efficiency of a heat pump is gauged in two ways. When the system acts like an air conditioner, you measure its efficiency in terms of the EER. When the pump behaves like a heat-producer, you evaluate efficiency by determining the *coefficient of performance* (COP). This factor is simply the amount of energy the pump gives off divided by the amount of energy the pump eats up in the process. (It's just another kind of EER.) If your heat pump gobbles up 10,000 Btu of electricity and puts out 20,000 Btu of heat, you have a COP of 2, a typical rating. For every dollar you spend on electricity, you get two bucks worth of warmth. Why, that's an efficiency of 200%, an efficiency that no fossil-fuel system could match. Even electric furnaces can't do any better than 100%. You already know the secret to the heat pump's astounding track record: the system simply uses electricity to *collect* heat, not *generate* it.

Most heat pumps can deliver a COP of 1.5 to 2.5, but their EER's are no better than those of conventional air conditioners. This means that with most pumps, you can get 1.5 to 2.5 times more heat from a given quantity of electricity than you could get from any electric furnace, but you can't expect to lower your cooling bills with a heat pump. The big savings roll in when the pump does your heating, above the balance point.

Cost

Heat pumps don't come cheap. A typical air-to-air unit costs $2000, not including ductwork and installation. That's more than the price of a gas or oil furnace plus an electric air conditioner. Some experts say you should expect a payback period of 4 years; others say it's closer to 10 years. I say don't make up your mind about heat pumps until you've looked at more than the price tags. You shouldn't forget that there are hundreds of thousands of people out there who own heat pumps, and most of those folks are reaping substantial savings on their heating bills. You have to juggle all the variables—your climate, the balance point, the cost of fuel, your budget. But you don't have to juggle alone. You can consult your utility company, friends who have heat pumps, and trustworthy heating contractors.

THE AIRTIGHT WOOD STOVE

Wood heat is making a comeback. There are hundreds of different wood stoves in the marketplace, and there are thousands more wood-stove owners every year who are whittling down their annual fuel bills. As long as energy prices are sky high, the trend will continue.

So it is only right that we discuss the most respected wood-burner on the scene: the modern airtight wood stove. After all, its heating efficiency rivals that of many conventional heating plants, achieving ratings of 40 to 65%. And the technology of the airtight wood stove is far more sophisticated than its run-of-the-mill wood-stove cousins.

This is a book on conserving fuel, so we will *not* dwell on that other much-admired wood-burner, the fireplace. It's charming, it's traditional, and *it's wasteful.* It sends about 90% of its heat right up the chimney. Nor will we review all those cousins—conventional wood stoves, antique wood stoves, "Franklin" stoves, and others. They, too, squander energy, with efficiencies of 40% or less. These wood-eaters are loved because of their heritage or their profile or their mood-making power. No one ever seriously contended that they saved lots of money.

How It Works

What's the secret of the airtight wood stove's performance? Better design. If you could see how a fire behaves in both a non-airtight and an airtight, you'd understand how improved design makes such a big difference in efficiency. In a conventional wood stove, the blaze grows and grows, pumping heat into the room, flaming toward ever higher temperatures. It races on until you reduce the draft or the firewood is consumed. But cutting the draft doesn't work well enough or fast enough. Air leaking into the firebox from all sides lets the fire burn too quickly, despite your efforts to rein in the flames. And a fast burn is an inefficient burn. You waste fuel that can cost more than $100 per cord. Worse still, the air seepage forces rivers of heat to flow right up the chimney, dragging warm house air with it.

Another problem is that to get the most from a wood fire, you have to burn two things: (1) gases given off by the wood as it heats up, and (2) the solid residue left after the gases disappear. Believe it or not, the gases constitute about half of wood's value as fuel, and they can't burn unless there's an extra supply of air *above* the fuel bed. Most of the air pouring into a non-airtight stove comes in near the base of the fire and drives the combustion of the solid residue. Primary air, it's called. The design of the non-airtight doesn't allow for the introduction of air above the base (called secondary air) so the gases can burn.

But get your fire going in an airtight and see how it fares. Right off you'll see the reason for the name: there are precious few air leaks. No, an airtight is not really airtight, but it's close enough to make a difference. Because there's little seepage, the fire can burn slowly and evenly, hour after hour. The flames respond promptly to the draft control. You get the proper amount of heat over long hauls, and that kind of combustion extracts more Btu's from your wood. And less air leakage means less air rushing up the chimney, pulling room heat to the outdoors. Plus, there's that little feature which has become one of the hallmarks of airtight technology: secondary air inlets. They make sure that air gets to those gases over the fuel bed, and the result is a money-saving explosion of Btu's.

How It's Made

All airtights are *not* alike. Yes, they have common design features, but there's also great variety throughout the species. The most obvious differences lie in appearance. Some airtights look like cast-iron treasure chests

Fig. 6-4. The Jøtul No. 118B holds logs up to 2 feet long and can be vented from the back or either side. The stove was first developed nearly 40 years ago.

Fig. 6-6. The Ashley Model C-60D heats four or five average rooms, takes logs up to 2 feet long, and has a thermostatically controlled air intake.

Fig. 6-5. The Old Mill OM-75 is made of ¼-inch-thick welded steel plate, has double loading doors and a side ash door, and burns coal as well as wood.

Fig. 6-7. The Old Mill OM-55 Slip-in comes with a solid metal shield to close off the fireplace opening.

(Figure 6-4); some, like old-time bank safes (Figure 6-5); some, like the console of a heavy-duty stereo system (Figure 6-6). A few are made to plug the energy-wasting jaws of fireplaces (Figure 6-7). It seems like everywhere you look you see an airtight with a different face.

There's plenty of variation on the inside of airtights, too. Many models, like the one show in Figure 6-4, have internal baffles to promote better combustion. Several airtights, notably the Ashley shown in Figure 6-6, have double "walls." The outer one is an attractive metal jacket, the inner one is the firebox, and the space between them is an air-heating chamber. Heat radiates from the firebox, warms the air that circulates into the chamber, and wafts out into the living space through vents in the jacket. Natural convection does most of the work. Such a stove is called a *circulating* type, to distinguish it from most other wood-burners, which warm by radiating heat from the wall of the firebox.

What It Can Do

Regardless of how nice the airtights' design or looks are, the bottom line is still what the wood-burners can do for you and your house. To find that out, you have to evaluate individual stoves and heating situations. Here are a few generalizations that may help. First of all, you'll find that airtights are more than little space heaters. All models can at least heat a room, some can heat several rooms, and a few can heat a small house. The maximum safe output for most airtights is about 15,000 to 45,000 Btuh. An electric space heater provides only about 5000 Btuh. Second, most airtights can burn up to at least 9 hours. If you detest cold stoves on winter mornings and want to stoke as little as possible, these long burners are on your side. Third, if you have a source of cheap wood or if the price of your conventional heat is out of sight, an airtight stove may decrease your heating bills significantly. For example, let's say last year you used 1200 gallons of heating oil at $1.24 a gallon (the national average price), which gave you an annual heating bill of $1488. To be more specific, what you bought was 109,200,000 Btu (1200 gallons × 91,000 Btu of useful heat in each gallon = 109,200,000 Btu). So this year you switch to wood heat and a big airtight stove. Since the wood you use has about 30,000,000 Btu per cord and your airtight is 50% efficient, you get approximately 15,000,000 Btu of useful heat from each cord you burn. And that means you need over 7 cords to match the heat output you had last year (109,200,000 Btu ÷ 15,000,000 Btu per cord = 7.28 cords). At $100 a cord (a good price for wood in many areas) your fuel bill this year would be $728 (7.28 cords $\times$ $100 per cord = $728). Annual savings due to your airtight: $1488 − $728 = $760. If the price of wood were higher or the cost of your conventional heat lower, the savings would be less. If you have a source of free wood, like your own woodlot, the savings would be almost sinful.

Alas, airtight stoves are not for everyone. To use an airtight you have to give up both space in your house to accommodate the wood-burner and space in your yard to store the wood. You have to apply considerable elbow grease to stack, split, and carry the fuelwood. You have to dispose of the ashes, sweep the chimney clear of creosote twice each heating season, stoke the fire, adjust the controls, and monitor the burning. You have to rigidly adhere to the rules of safe stove operation. Too many homeowners have caused too many fires by being just a little too careless with their wood-burning stoves. And, or course, you have to confront the price tag. In general, the better stoves cost over $300; some cost over $700.

If none of these facts dissuade you from seriously considering an airtight, stay on the trail. Seek advice from wood-stove dealers and owners, read pertinent books and periodicals, check with your building code officials. And when you shop, look for the smallest stove required to heat your space, insist on stoves made of heavy cast iron or $\frac{1}{8}$-inch-thick plate steel, prefer fireboxes with firebrick linings and solid joints, demand stove doors that seal tightly, and expect air inlets that adjust easily but hold their setting firmly.

THE KEROSENE HEATER

I can't think of a domestic energy-saver that's more thoroughly shrouded in controversy than the modern kerosene space heater. Some homeowners swear by this heat-maker; others fear it. Some authorities frown on it; others grant it an approving smile. Lots of people crow about the heater's high efficiency, its ability to slash heating bills, its safety-conscious design, and others are talking about its hazards. What's the real story?

On the positive side, modern kerosene heaters really do have important safety features. Unlike old-time kerosene heaters (the barometric types), today's models are wick-fed and unpressurized, making them a world safer than their dangerous and smelly forbears. If the flame goes out on a wick-fed model, the fuel stops feeding, greatly reducing the risk of fire. The best new-fangled heaters also have automatic shut-off devices that extinguish the flame if the heaters are jarred or tipped. Electric lighting systems in the better heaters eliminate the need to use matches to light the units. And because of improved burner design, state-of-the-art kerosene heaters give you combustion so thorough that there is little or no odor, smoke, or fuel emissions, when you operate the unit properly. It's not surprising then that many contemporary heaters are UL listed.

And it really is true that these modern heaters can save you money. They're so efficient at yanking Btu's out of a gallon of kerosene that they can provide cheaper heat than either oil or electric heating plants. Homeowners take advantage of the heaters' exceptional performance by setting their home thermostats way back and warming only a few areas of the house with the heaters.

Perhaps the supreme example of current heater technology is the Kero-Sun line (Figure 6-8). These units have an efficiency rating of 99.9%, carry the UL listing mark, have heating capacities ranging from 8200 to 19,500 Btuh, burn 13 to 39 hours on a single tank of fuel (1 to 2 gallons), weigh 14 to 35 pounds, and cost $150 to $290. They have all the safety features I mentioned plus a few more, including a low center of gravity for greater stability, an accessory siphon pump that permits safe tank-filling without a mess, and oil-proof rubber seals throughout to prevent leaks. Kero-Sun claims that their heaters are smokeless and odorless.

But the other side of the coin reveals that there have been problems associated with kerosene heaters, safety features or not. Kerosene heaters have caused some house fires. And every heater on the market has the potential of depleting too much oxygen in a room and producing too much carbon monoxide, if the system is handled improperly. It's no secret that in certain parts of the country kerosene space heaters are banned.

So are these superefficient heat-makers really dangerous? As far as I can see, there is no evidence to suggest that modern kerosene heaters are inherently hazardous. But they can be dangerous if they're handled incorrectly. The heaters "cause" house fires because people use the wrong fuel or position the units too close to curtains and other flammables or handle the fuel improperly or commit some other insane act. Serious oxygen depletion or carbon monoxide poisoning happens when people don't correctly ventilate the heaters. They forget that no matter how clean burning the kerosene heater is, it still requires a slightly opened window for adequate ventilation. Vented or not, the heater *must have* that extra draft.

Fig. 6-8. Kero-Sun portable kerosene heaters with the Model K stainless steel cookstove (bottom center).

The bottom line is that a kerosene heater can be a noble warrior in the battle against rising fuel prices, but you have to respect the system's potential for harm. Respect means operating a heater by the book:

- Burn only water-clear 1-K kerosene. *Never* use gasoline, white gas, campstove fuel, or anything else. Yellow kerosene smokes, smells, and fouls up the heater works. Gasoline in a kerosene heater is a fire bomb.
- Store kerosene in the proper metal container. Don't ever use a plastic container.
- In the room where the heater is operating, *always open a window at*

least 1 inch, regardless of whether the system is vented to the outdoors.

- Keep children away from those heaters whose surfaces get hot.
- Position heaters away from all combustible materials—curtains, furniture, clothes, etc.
- Never use heaters in bathrooms, laundry rooms, or other enclosed spaces.
- Consult your building and fire officials for information on code requirements and safety.

CHAPTER
SEVEN

Saving Money With
Your Appliances and Lights

Consider an "average" family of four and their "typ-ical" house humming with appliances, lit by the almighty watt. How much money do you think they could save each year if they made an all-out effort to conserve gadget and light energy? $50? $100? Let's see. Their yearly electrical usage is 7500 kilowatt-hours (kWh), at a cost of about 6¢ per unit. That comes to $450 yearly. If they cut their annual usage by one-third (an easy job for most families), they'd save *$150 a year.* Nothing to sneeze at. Why, in 20 years they'd be $3000 to the good. And that doesn't take into account the effects of rising fuel prices. If the utility company hiked unit costs just 6% a year, the 20-year savings would be $5519!

So let's bury forever the notion that money saved from efficient use of appliances and lights is insignificant. The fact is, most homeowners can make a small fortune through appliance and light conservation. After all, in most homes there's a lot to work with. Believe it or not, the "average" household has at least 50 appliances, and about as many lights. And the investment required in time and money to make that modest fortune is usually meager, if not microscopic.

THE *REAL* COST OF APPLIANCES AND LIGHTS

You're in your local appliance store shopping for a new refrigerator. You fall in love with two brand-name units that seem nearly identical, just different manufacturers and price tags. One costs $500; the other, $450.

Which is the better buy? If you fed that question into a computer, you would get a printout that says, "Insufficient data. Cannot compute." And part of the reason is that the purchase price is only a small portion of the real cost of an appliance. The big factor is operating costs. As the energy squeeze gets worse, we're constantly reminded that it nearly always costs more to run an applicance or light than to buy one.

When we consider the purchase price *and* operating costs of a device that consumes energy, we're doing *life-cycle costing*. We do it before we buy a house, calculating how much it's going to cost each year to heat the place. We do it when we shop for a new car, eyeing the EPA gas mileage sticker to see if we can afford to feed the beast. And soon we may find ourselves doing it at every turn to help us measure the true costs of wasteful appliances and the real savings of energy-efficient living.

It is easy to calculate the operating costs of an energy-eater. Consider an electric self-cleaning range. This one has an especially big appetite, consuming an average of 1667 kWh a year. At a utility rate of 6¢ per kWh, that appetite costs the owner $100 annually. If fuel prices stayed the same, the lifetime operating cost of the range would be $100 times the number of years the owner uses it. In 20 years the range's total operating cost would be $2000. But we know that in the real world fuel prices *don't* remain constant; they rise with a vengeance. To calculate the effects of this fuel inflation on operating costs, you have to have a head for figures, or an inflation computer like the one in Table 7-1. It tells you the cumulative cost to operate an energy-using device for a given number of years at a given fuel inflation rate. (The table will work for other annual expenses, too, like rent, food bills, medical costs, anything subject to inflationary price increases.) The table is based on an initial-year operating cost of $100, but it's easy to make the table accommodate any other amount. And the "initial year" can be any year you care to start with. So to determine the real-world operating cost of that self-cleaning range (with $100 initial-year operating cost) for 20 years at 6% annual inflation, just find 20 years in the "lifetime" column, scan to the 6% inflation column, and read the bad news: $3679.

Obviously, to estimate the initial-year operating cost of one of your appliances or lights, you must know the gadget's average annual energy usage and your energy unit cost. Table 7-2 will help you with the former; your utility bills will help you determine the latter. If you select several recent utility bills, add up their charges, sum their units of fuel usage (kWh's, cubic feet, etc.), and divide the total charges by the total fuel units,

Table 7-1
Lifetime Operating Cost for Every $100 of First-Year Cost

Lifetime in Years	Annual Fuel Inflation Rate, %							
	0	2	4	6	8	10	15	20
1	100	100	100	100	100	100	100	100
2	200	202	204	206	208	210	215	220
3	300	306	312	318	325	331	347	364
5	500	520	542	564	587	611	674	744
8	800	858	921	990	1,064	1,144	1,373	1,650
10	1,000	1,095	1,201	1,318	1,449	1,594	2,030	2,596
15	1,500	1,729	2,002	2,328	2,715	3,177	4,758	7,204
20	2,000	2,430	2,978	3,679	4,576	5,727	10,244	18,669
25	2,500	3,203	4,165	5,468	7,311	9,835	21,279	47,198
30	3,000	4,057	5,608	7,906	11,328	16,449	43,475	118,188
35	3,500	4,999	7,365	11,143	17,232	27,102	88,117	294,834
40	4,000	6,040	9,503	15,476	25,906	44,259	177,909	734,386
50	5,000	8,458	15,267	29,034	57,377	116,391	721,772	4,549,719

Source: *Conserve Energy and Save Money* by John Elvans Smith, 1981. Used with the permission of McGraw-Hill Book Company.

you'll get your average unit cost. Annual usage times unit cost equals initial-year operating cost.

Choosing a reasonable fuel inflation rate shouldn't be any problem either. It's hard to open a newspaper without coming across those annoying percentages. When I chose 6% in the preceding example, I was being conservative. There are those who think that a 10% annual fuel inflation rate will be the norm for the eighties.

To use Table 7-1 for an initial-year operating cost of less or more than $100, use fractions. According to Table 7-2, an electric hand iron uses about 144 kWh a year. At 6¢ per kWh, that's an annual operating cost of $8.64. Over a lifetime of 20 years, with an average inflation rate of 10%, the hand iron will achieve an operating cost of 8.64/100 × $5727 = $494.81. That $5727 is the 20-year operating cost (at 10% inflation) of any device with a $100 initial-year cost. And since the iron's initial-year cost is just a fraction of $100 (8.64/100), the 20-year cost is a fraction of $5727 (8.64/100). The same law of proportions applies to a gadget with an initial-year cost of *more* than $100. If your device cost $246 to run the first year, you'd multiply the values in Table 7-1 by 246/100.

Table 7-2
Annual Energy Requirements of Electric Household Appliances.

	Estimated kWh used Annually		*Estimated kWh used Annually*
MAJOR APPLIANCES		**HEATING AND COOLING**	
Air-conditioner (room)[1]	860	Air cleaner	216
Clothes dryer	993	Electric blanket	147
Dishwasher, including energy to		Dehumidifier	377
heat water	2,110	Fan, attic	291
Dishwasher only	363	Fan, circulating	43
Freezer, (16. cu. ft.)	1,190	Fan, rollaway	138
Freezer, frostless (16.5 cu. ft.)	1,820	Fan, window	170
Range with oven	700	Heater, portable	176
Range with self-cleaning oven	730	Heating pad	10
Refrigerator (12 cu. ft.)	728	Humidifier	163
Refrigerator, frostless (12 cu. ft.)	1,217		
Refrigerator/freezer (12.5 cu. ft.)	1,500	**HEALTH & BEAUTY**	
Refrigerator/freezer, frostless		Germicidal lamp	141
(17.5 cu. ft.)	2,250	Hair dryer	14
Washing machine, automatic	2,500	Heat lamp, infrared	13
including energy to heat		Shaver	1.8
water		Sun lamp	16
washing machine only	103	Toothbrush	0.5
Washing machine, nonautomatic	2,497	Vibrator	2
including energy to heat		**HOME ENTERTAINMENT**	
water		Radio	86
washing machine only	76	Radio/record player	109
Water heater	4,811	Television; b/w, tube type	350
		Television, b/w, solid state	120
KITCHEN APPLIANCES		Television, color, tube type	660
Blender	15	Television, color, solid state	440
Broiler	100		
Carving knife	8	**HOUSEWARES**	
Coffee maker	140	Clock	17
Deep fryer	83	Floor polisher	15
Egg cooker	14	Sewing machine	11
Frying pan	186	Vacuum cleaner	46
Hot plate	90	Iron, hand	144
Mixer	13		
Microwave oven	190		
Roaster	205		
Sandwich grill	33		
Toaster	39		
Trash compactor	50		
Waffle iron	22		
Waste disposer	30		

Source: U.S. Department of Energy.
[1]Based on 1000 hours of operation per year. This figure will vary widely depending on geographic area and specific size of unit.

BIG APPLIANCES, BIG SAVINGS

If you've read Table 7-2 carefully, you know where most of your appliance energy is going. Not into the waffle iron, hair dryer, or vacuum cleaner, but into the *big* machines—the refrigerator, range, clothes dryer, dishwasher, clothes washer, and the like. In a "typical" four-person household, the refrigerator gobbles up 22% of the year's electricity; the electric range, 14%; the clothes dryer, 12%; the dishwasher, 4%; the washer, 2%. But the plus side of the story is that those big appetites can usually be curbed in big ways. It's a law of energy saving economics: the greater the use of energy, the better the prospects for conservation.

In the next few pages you'll see how to apply that law to the "big five" appliances just mentioned. You'll learn how to use them efficiently, how to make them save you money. You'll get some tips on how to weed out the efficient units from the duds when you're shopping around. And you'll discover that conserving appliance energy is easy on your lifestyle.

Refrigerators and Freezers

The most obvious and most neglected rule of efficient refrigerator operation is "Keep the door shut as much as possible." Whenever you open the door, cool air falls out, warm air wafts in, and the motor has to work overtime to get your fridge's interior temperature back to normal. Nothing can increase your refrigerator's operating cost faster than a lot of unnecessary door-flapping. You might try keeping an up-to-date inventory of your refrigerator's contents and posting the list in the kitchen. That way, you wouldn't have to open the fridge door to find out what's inside. And before preparing a meal, remove from the refrigerator everything you'll need, and put things back all at once after mealtime. The savings could be significant. All this door talk applies to freezers and freezer compartments, too.

A fully loaded refrigerator or freezer operates more efficiently than a partially full or nearly empty one. A full compartment doesn't hold as much cold air as an empty one, and therefore doesn't lose as much cold when you open its door. Also, your refrigerated food retains cold and actually makes things easier on the motor. So as long as there's enough room in your compartments for cold air to circulate evenly, fill 'er up.

But don't fill it up with hot foods. They'll warm up the refrigerated air and everything else, too, and the cooling mechanism will have to kick in to compensate. Let things cool down before you pop them in a cold compartment. You can let hot food stand for 15 or 20 minutes without having to worry about bacteria.

If the temperature in your refrigerator, freezer section, or freezer isn't right, you could be wasting a lot of energy and a lot of money. Maybe $50 a year, maybe more. Your fridge should have a temperature of 38 to 40°F; your freezer or freezer section, 0° (for long-term storage) to 5°F (for normal chilling). If you're not sure about the temperature in one of your food chillers, put an outdoor thermometer you can trust in there with Monday's dinner. If the temperature is wrong, adjust the control dial, wait, and take another reading. A few minutes of this kind of trial and error should set things right.

A bad door gasket on a refrigeration appliance is bad news. Cold air leaks out; operating costs go up. To see if your door gasket is airtight, close the door on a dollar bill. If you can easily slip the bill out, replace or adjust the gasket. If there's plenty of drag on the bill, keep checking—test around the rest of the door.

Frost buildup in your freezer reduces cooling efficiency. The frost acts as insulation, impeding the transfer of cold from cooling mechanism to compartment, making the motor's job tougher. On manual-defrost models, keep the frost down to $\frac{1}{4}$ inch thick or less.

Where is your refrigerator or freezer? If it's near a stove, a dishwasher, or a heating vent, it's probably using more energy than it has to. And if it's in a sunny spot, it could be working itself to death. Warm temperatures outside a refrigerated compartment make it harder for cooling mechanisms to maintain cold temperatures inside. So if you can, place your fridge or freezer in the coolest part of a room, with lots of air circulation.

Dust and lint that collect on your unit's heat-exchange (condenser) coils or fins cut cooling efficiency. Those devices dispel the heat extracted from food in the cooling compartment. And when they're dirty, they may as well be coated with insulation. Heat isn't expelled as it should be and the whole machine has to work harder. Every three months unplug the beast and vacuum those coils or fins with a brush attachment. You may find them on the back of your unit or behind the front access panel near the floor (Figure 7-1). If you have trouble identifying them, check your owner's manual.

When you shop for a new refrigerator or freezer, remember that frostless models are energy hogs. Look at Table 7-2 and see for yourself: manual-

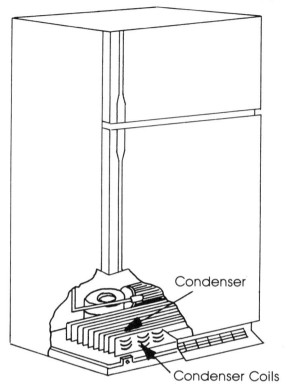

Fig. 7-1. Refrigerator condensor coils.

defrost refrigerator (12 cubic feet), 728 kWh per year; frostless refrigerator (12 cubic feet), 1217 kWh a year. That's a difference of 489 kWh annually, which can translate into as much as $50 a year, just for the luxury of not having to defrost by hand. In 20 years, with an average inflation rate of 10%, that frostless feature could cost you $2864!

In refrigeration appliances, as in houses, well placed insulation is golden. It should be the first energy saving feature you look for when buying a new appliance. Too many refrigerators have only about an inch of fiberglass insulation in the outer shell. There should be three times as much. No doubt you'll pay more for extra insulation, but every dime you invest in additional heat-stoppers will return to you tenfold in lowered operating costs.

When looking for a new refrigerator, it's worth considering the "power-saver switch," found on a lot of newer models. It lets you control the heaters in the doors and walls. The heaters are designed to prevent condensation, or "sweating," on the outer surfaces. Those heaters don't need to be on much of the time, so the power-saver switch allows you to shut them down when you want. That shutdown option can cut 16% off energy costs. But you should know that the switch is *not* an example of conservation technology at its best. Far from it. You see, the heaters controlled by the switch would be unnecessary if enough insulation were installed in the doors and walls. Because there's so little heat-retarding material in the outer shells, that cold from the inside gets to the outside, causing condensation to set up on outer surfaces. To beat the sweating, manufacturers try to beat the chill with heaters. So the power-saver option saves energy that shouldn't be used in the first place.

Ever wonder why chest-type freezers are so much more popular than upright freezers? One reason is that the chests don't lose a lot of cold air every time they're opened. Cold air falls; hot air rises. When you swing open the door of an upright, cold air spills out toward the floor, and warm air moves in.

Refrigerator/freezers should have two doors: one for the fridge, one for the freezer. That way, you don't have to open (and therefore warm) both compartments when you want to get at just one.

Casters and removable grills are always good to have on any fridge or freezer, because they make it easier to clean condenser coils and fins.

Ranges and Ovens

The first principle of energy-efficient cooking is "Always match fuel usage to the cooking task." That means making every Btu count, using precisely the energy you need, and no more, every time you turn on your stove. At its simplest level, the principle asks that we adopt some important habits: cooking with covered pans, cutting food into smaller pieces so it'll cook faster, baking several foods together, cooking with as little water as possible, thawing foods before trying to heat them up, matching pan sizes to the burners so less heat is lost to the air, using small cooking appliances (hot plates, electric frying pans, etc.) whenever we can, trying not to open the oven door while food is baking, shutting burners off just before food is done to let residual heat finish the job, cooking oven roasts at 325°F, avoiding oven preheating, and using the range-top rather than the oven whenever possible.

Maintenance is an important part of getting the most from your oven and range. The easiest place to start is at the reflectors beneath the surface burners. Keep them clean and shiny and they'll be able to reflect maximum heat up to your pots and pans. If you have a gas stove, make sure that burner and pilot flames burn blue, not yellow. Blue means efficient burning; yellow means wasted fuel. Check your owner's manual for flame adjustment procedures. And, keep the burners spotless. Dirty ones are inefficient and occasionally hazardous.

When it comes to saving fuel, your cookware can be as important as your cooking habits. Copper, aluminum, and cast-iron pans conduct heat well, so they make good use of a burner's Btu's. Flat-bottom cookware absorbs a lot more heat from a burner than round-bottom types. And ceramic or glass cooking utensils retain heat longer than metal ones. Choose the right pan and you can turn the heat down.

Are microwave ovens energy-savers? The answer has to be yes—and no. Microwave ovens can cook *most* foods faster and therefore more economically than conventional ovens. But most is not all. For example, a microwave oven uses 30% more energy than a regular oven to cook frozen broccoli; 46% more for peas; 58% more for summer squash.

When you're looking to buy a new range or oven, remember that gas ranges and ovens shouldn't have pilot lights—they should have automatic (electronic) ignition systems. Pilot lights burn continuously, consuming gas even when you're not cooking; automatic ignition systems ignite the burners with a spark only when you need the heat. So go electronic and save up to 47% on your gas usage.

Keep an eye on insulation. Most conventional ovens have about $1\frac{1}{2}$ inches of fiberglass insulation, and that just isn't enough. Too many Btu's are wasted. The self-cleaning (pyrolytic) ovens, however, have about twice as much fiberglass stuffing. So as long as you use the self-cleaning feature sparingly, you'll come out ahead.

Use the activating self-clean only when absolutely necessary and only immediately after baking to give the oven a head start on reaching the high temperature required for cleaning.

Oven doors with windows are money savers. Every time you open your oven to see how things are cooking, the interior temperature drops 25 to 50°F. A see-through door lets you look without wasting.

Dishwashers

The biggest expense in running a dishwasher is hot water. A normal wash requires about 15 gallons, all heated, with your money, to way over

100°F. Fortunately, the simplest conservation tricks make the biggest difference in your machine's yearly hot water usage. These tricks include always washing full loads, using the right amount of dishwasher detergent, pre-rinsing your dishes by hand in cold water, loading the washer according to instructions in your owner's manual, and skipping the "rinse and hold" cycle. All this fussing could save you $100 a year.

A simple way to cut your machine's use of electricity is to cancel out the drying cycle after the final rinse, open the door, and let the air do the drying. Using the electric heater costs a lot of kilowatts. Savings from thin air: $5 to $30 a year.

The closer your dishwasher is to your water heater, the less heat your water line will lose. A short hose is an efficient hose.

Your owner's manual probably says that you should use water that's 140 to 160°F. But the fact is, your machine may clean beautifully with 120°F water. If you can get by with the lower temperature, you might save $100 a year. So experiment with your water heater thermostat. If your machine doesn't clean well with the lower temp, blame the detergent first.

Two maintenance chores should be standard operating procedure: cleaning the heating element and cleaning out the filter screen over the drain (Figure 7-2). Unless you regularly file or scrape off the white deposits on the heating element, it will do a lousy job of putting heat into the water. And if you don't remove food particles from the filter screen every week, the works will clog and efficiency will drop.

Shopping for energy-saving dishwashers means looking for energy-saving cycles. For example, a "light wash" cycle (for lightly soiled dishes) can save you as much as $50 a year in hot water, electricity, and detergent. A "short wash" cycle (for all but the very dirtiest dishes) uses only about 10 gallons of hot water per wash. And an "air dry" cycle automatically shuts down the machine after the final rinse to let Mother Nature do the drying. The feature can slash 10% off your dishwasher energy costs.

Washing Machines

According to Table 7-2, an automatic clothes washer uses about 2500 kWh annually—only 103 kWh to run the machine, but 2397 kWh just to heat the water! So like your dishwasher, your washing machine needs all the help it can get in hot water conservation. Therefore, wash only full loads unless you can adjust the machine's water level, use warm or cold water for washing and cold for rinsing (studies show that most clothes washed in cold

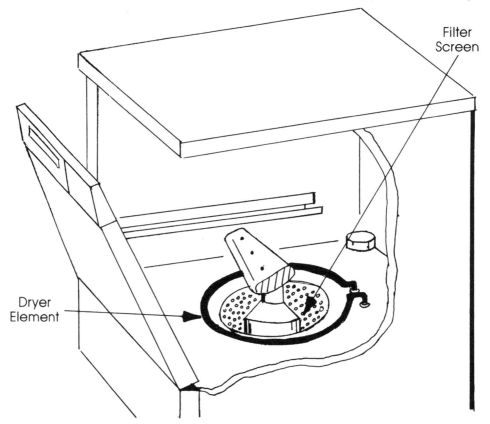

Fig. 7-2. The two dishwasher components that deserve the most attention—week after week.

water are about as clean as those washed in warm), and presoak especially dirty clothes rather than try to purge them with hot water.

To save washer electricity, use the right amount of detergent (over-sudsing overworks your machine; undersudsing makes you rewash) and match wash cycles to the clothes (delicate fabrics come clean in short cycles; heavier clothes require longer ones).

The short-hose principle applies to your washing machine as well as your dishwasher. If you're committed to hot washes and warm rinses, a shorter water line can save you thousands of Btu's a year.

When you're in the market for a new washer, you'll be well-served by a front-loading model with adjustable water levels and a "suds saver" feature. Front-loading machines use less hot water than top-loaders. True, they cost more, but they'll save you money over the long haul. The adjustable water levels help you conserve hot water. Pressure-filled models control the water level better than the timed-fill units. That suds saver feature is a smart investment. It lets you use the same batch of hot water on several loads. You wash the cleaner clothes first, then the dirtier loads. The device can cut a washer's hot water usage in half.

Clothes Dryers

Without investing a single penny, without tinkering with your dryer, without giving up anything, you can cut your drying costs by at least 75%. Maybe more. It's all in how you do your drying. A handful of simple (and patently obvious) procedures can make some impressive dents in your operating costs. First, dry your clothes in a quick succession of loads to take advantage of the heat built up in the dryer, set the timer to the *minimum* time needed to dry the load, dry heavy and light fabrics separately so you can match drying times to the "dryability" of the loads, use the fluff-air feature if your dryer has one, run full (not oversized) loads, and solar-dry your clothes every chance you get—with your clothesline.

To keep repairs from costing you a fortune, you have to clean the lint screens after each load and the exhaust vents every six months. A clogged screen works your dryer extra hard, lengthens drying time, and puts a strain on the heating coils. A dirty vent is just as bad—it makes your dryer gobble up more energy than it really needs.

Place your dryer in a warm area for the same reason you put your fridge in a cool one: outside temperatures affect inside temperatures. So in the winter an unheated garage or utility room is no place for the machine that treats your clothes with hot air.

Vent your electric dryer *indoors* in winter and you'll get more use out of all those Btu's you pay for. To get extra heat and moisture without extra expense, just disconnect the exhaust hose from your wall vent, cover the mouth of the hose with cheesecloth to trap lint, and plug the wall vent with insulation to retard heat loss from the house. To be on the safe side, get your serviceman to check your work. You want him to ensure that your new setup doesn't alter the pressure in the exhaust system too much, because a big change could damage the heating element. Caution: You probably should *not* vent a gas dryer indoors because combustion gases travel with the warm air through the exhaust hose. Some local building codes ban the practice.

When you shop for a dryer, don't overlook energy saving controls. A moisture-sensing shutoff control gives a dryer some smarts so that the machine runs only when clothes are damp and shuts down when they're dry. An adjustable thermostat lets you control drying temperature so you can manage those Btu's better.

THE ART OF SENSIBLE LIGHTING

There are two ways to change any lighting situation: manipulate the source of the light or manipulate the environment. When you replace a 100-watt incandescent bulb with a 25-watt fluorescent light, or reduce the lighting in a room to a more comfortable level, you're manipulating the source, for the better. When you use translucent lampshades, or paint the walls a lighter color, or open the curtains on a sunny day, you're tinkering with the environment. When you manipulate both to your advantage, your lighting costs take a nose dive.

Managing the Source: Watts and Lumens

How much do you really know about your lighting sources? Answer true or false to the following:

1. Light bulbs of equal wattage give off equal light.
2. Three bulbs with a combined rating of 100 watts illuminate better than one 100-watt bulb.
3. Less light always means more lighting efficiency.
4. Incandescent (tungsten) bulbs are cheaper to operate than fluorescent tubes.

If you said true to any of those statements, look again. They're *all* false. Which proves that sorting out the why's and wherefore's of lighting sources isn't the easiest thing in the world. That is, unless you have a solid understanding of the relationship between watts and lumens.

A watt is a gauge of how much electricity a device uses. A lumen is a measure of how much light a source produces. You can have a 100-watt lamp that gives off 1700 lumens, or a 50-watt lamp that beams forth 3400 lumens—twice as much light. You can have sources with identical wattage and completely different lumens ratings. Or vice versa. For efficient lighting, scrutinize *both* watts and lumens.

Matching each household task to the proper degree of lighting (the right number of lumens) is the first big step you have to take. You'll probably save a lot of watts—and some strain on your eyes. Table 7-3 shows recommended lumens for certain tasks. You'll find the lumens for each of your lights printed on the bulb or tube or on the original package. The trick is, obviously, to get the correct lighting level at the lowest possible wattage.

As you try to work out that watts/lumens balance, you'll notice that incandescent bulbs of high wattage are more efficient than those of lower wattage. A 150-watt bulb gives off about 2900 lumens; two 75-watters produce only about 2300 lumens. So the one source costs you just as much as the pair but gives you 26% more light. You'll find a similar discrepancy in lumens output between incandescent and fluorescent lights. A 60-watt incandescent yields 840 lumens, but a 60-watt fluorescent gives you about *3360 lumens.* The fluorescents always give you more light per dollar than Edison's finest, and they last up to ten times as long.

You'll also uncover the truth about long-life and frosted bulbs. The long-lifes owe their longevity to inefficiency: They burn on and on because they give off less light per watt than standard incandescent bulbs. They may save you the inconvenience of a lot of bulb-changing in hard-to-get-at places, but they won't save you energy. And neither will frosted bulbs. The "frosting" is designed to *reduce* the lumens. That's why a clear 4-watt night light gives you about as much light as a frosted 7-watter—and costs you about half as much to use.

The yardstick of a light's efficiency is clearly the lumens/watt ratio. It tells you how many lumens a light produces per watt of electricity. Incan-

Table 7-3

Recommended Lumens for Specific Tasks

Task	Lumens
Reading, writing, studying	70
Playing cards, billiards, table tennis	30
Shaving, combing hair, applying makeup	50
Working in the kitchen	50–70
Laundering, ironing	50
Sewing, low-contrast dark fabrics	200
Sewing, light- to medium-colored fabrics	100
Sewing for short periods of time	50
Close handicraft work (reading blueprints, checking diagrams, finishing furniture)	100
Cabinetmaking (planing, cutting, sanding, gluing, measuring)	50

Source: Courtesy Butterick Publishing.

Size 30"x 30" Unusual use by architects Elder, Angell and Lange.

Fig. 7-3. A skylight illuminates this bedroom dressing table and sheds a good deal of light on the rest of the living space as well. (Courtesy Ventarama Skylight Corporation)

descent bulbs, for example, have an efficiency of 8 to 23 lumens per watt. Fluorescents, as you would expect, rate much higher—42 to 84 lumens per watt. The ratio will come in handy every time you find yourself scratching your head over which bulb or tube to buy, especially when you're shopping for offbeat lighting. Do some fast division and you'll discover that sodium vapor outdoor lamps are super-efficient (95 to 140 lumens per watt), that high-intensity discharge (HID) reading lamps give you plenty of light at low cost (29 to 105 lumens per watt), and that 50-watt reflector floodlights in pole or spot lamps beat out 100-watt incandescents every time (about 34 lumens per watt).

I haven't mentioned the importance of turning off unnecessary lights because you know all about it. But you may not know about solid-state dimmers or high-low switches, which are convenient masters of watts *and* lumens. These gadgets can save you enough electricity to pay for themselves

Fig. 7-4. These two skylight units compensate for the paltry sunshine that creeps in the tree-shaded windows below. (Courtesy Ventarama Skylight Corporation)

in a year. Some of them go on the lamp cord; some of them replace the standard light switch on the wall; all of them let you manipulate lumens to save watts.

Managing the Environment

Let's pretend you have a bedroom lit by four 100-watt bulbs—three in the ceiling, one in a hanging lamp. The walls are olive, the two windows have dark floral curtains, the room is in the north end of the house, and those bulbs burn to the tune of $50 a year. Problem: How do you reduce the lighting costs of the room without buying new light fixtures?

Step 1: Paint the walls. If you were to slap some white enamel over that dark green, the 400-watts would nearly blind you. You'd have to get rid of one of the bulbs (and replace it with a burnt-out one for safety). Light reflects off light-colored surfaces better than dark ones, so the brighter your walls, the more good you'll get out of your lights.

Step 2: Replace those dreary curtains. You want light-colored curtains as well as bright walls. If you were to put up some bright pastels, you might be able to delete another bulb.

Step 3: Buy a more translucent lampshade. The lighter the color, the better. You'd be surprised how many more lumens you can get out of a lamp simply by switching shades.

Step 4: Swear never to try to read or knit by the lights from the ceiling. It's inefficient. If you bring that hanging lamp down close enough, you won't need as many watts overhead. This kind of "task lighting" is always a money-saver.

Step 5: Use the sun. Relocate the desk or dresser or chair to take full advantage of the free light. Try using mirrors to reflect daylight into the room. And consider putting in a skylight—the built-in light-giver for remodeled attics, inner bathrooms, and rooms on the north side (Figure 7-3). Nowadays, you can buy insulated skylights the way you buy storm windows—as complete, weatherproof building units (Figure 7-4). Even unhandy handymen can install one in a day.

The result of all this juggling of the lighting environment will be a savings of at least $25 a year, perhaps $30 or $40. And similar savings are possible throughout your own house.

Suggestions for Further Reading

GENERAL

Community Services Administration. *Save Energy: Save Money!* Washington D.C., 1977.

Editors of *Better Homes and Gardens. Better Homes and Gardens Home Plan Ideas,* Summer, 1980.

Hand, A. J. *Home Energy How-To.* Harper & Row, New York, 1977.

Jones, Peter. *How to Cut Heating and Cooling Costs.* New Century, New York, 1979.

Smith, John Elvans. *Conserve Energy and Save Money.* McGraw-Hill, New York, 1981.

Stroetzel, Donald and Dorothy. "How to Cut Your Home Energy Costs," *Reader's Digest,* September, 1981, 67–74.

U.S. Department of Agriculture. *Energy Management Checklist of the Home.* Washington, D.C., 1975.

U.S. Dpeartment of Energy. *Tips for Energy Savers.* Washington, D.C., 1978.

U.S. Department of Housing and Urban Development. *In the Bank ... Or up the Chimney?* Washington, D.C., 1977.

THERMAL INSULATION

Editors of Sunset Books and *Sunset Magazine. Do-It-Yourself Insulation and Weatherstripping.* Sunset Books, Menlo Park, California, 1979.

Meyers, L. Donald. *How to Do Your Own Home Insulating.* Harper & Row, New York, 1978.

NAHB Research Foundation, Inc. *Insulation Manual: Homes, Apartments.* Rockville, Maryland, 1979.

Oviatt, A. E., U.S. Department of Agriculture Forest and Range Experiment Station. *Optimum Insulation Thickness in Wood-Framed Homes.* Portland, Oregon, 1975.

Wing, Charlie and John Lyons. "Insulating Your Walls and Floors," *New Shelter,* September, 1980, 90–98.

WEATHERSTRIPPING AND CAULKING

Editors of *Consumer Reports.* "Exterior Caulking Compounds," *Consumer Reports,* May, 1976, 291–295.

Editors of *Consumer Reports.* "Exterior Caulking Compounds," *Consumer Reports,* October, 1981, 579–581.

Editors of Consumer Reports. "Weatherstripping," *Consumer Reports,* February, 1977, 110–112.

Editors of *Consumer Reports.* "Weatherstripping," *Consumer Reports,* October, 1981, 576–578.

Editors of Time-Life Books. "Keeping a House Snug and Tight," in *Weatherproofing.* Time-Life Books, Alexandria, Virginia, 1977.

WINDOWS AND DOORS

Adams, Jennifer A. "What to Look for in Window Insulation," *Solar Age,* January, 1982, 46–48.

Editors of *Consumer Reports.* "Storm Windows and Weatherstripping," *Consumer Reports,* October, 1978, 583.

Editors of *Consumer Reports.* "Window Insulators," *Consumer Reports,* October, 1981, 583–585.

Editors of *Solar Age.* "Window Insulation Directory," *Solar Age,* January, 1982, 49–55.

Hand, A. J. "Windows and Doors," in *Home Energy How-To.* Harper & Row, New York, 1977.

Lafavore, Michael. "The Trouble With Windows (and What to Do)," *New Shelter,* October, 1980, 26–29.

Rawlings, Roger. "A Mini-Catalog of Products," *New Shelter,* October, 1980, 36–38.

HEATING AND COOLING

Bear, David, "A Layman's Guide to Lower Oil Bills," *New Shelter,* October, 1980, 49–60.

U.S. Department of Agriculture. *Home Heating.* Washington, D.C. 1977.

U.S. Department of Energy. *Heating With Wood.* Washington, D.C., 1980.

Wade, Alex. "Heating and Cooling," in *A Design and Construction Handbook for Energy-Saving Houses.* Rodale Press, Inc., Emmaus, Pennsylvania, 1980.

Wing, Charlie. "Ways to Improve Your Heating System," *New Shelter,* January, 1981, 61–69.

APPLIANCES AND LIGHTS

Butel, Jane. "Saving Electricity With Household Appliances," *Journal of Home Economics*, November, 1975, 21.

Lovingood, Rebecca P. "Money Saving Tips for Home Appliances," in *Cutting Energy Costs: The 1980 Yearbook of Agriculture*. Washington, D.C., 1980.

Smith, John Elvans. "Appliances: Kilowatt-Hour Extravaganza," in *Conserve Energy and Save Money*. McGraw-Hill, New York, 1981.

U.S. Department of Energy. *How to Understand Your Utility Bill*. Washington, D.C., 1978.

Index